# LAUNCHING TO LEADING

"The Breakthrough mindset in *Launching to Leading* is for the whole business not just marketing. It's about thriving in the decade of disruption and staying relevant. It's about aligning the complexity of your offer, your core clients needs and at the same time differentiating your value. These three become the perfect storm for competitive advantage."

—**Matt Church**, Author, Founder,
Chairman Thought Leaders Global

"Messaging and positioning can make or break Marketing Automation ROI. Read this book, get it right, and get the most from your marketing technology investments."

—**Tom Grubb**, Chief Strategy Officer,
Digital Pi and Former VP of Product Marketing, Marketo

"A career's worth of theory and practical experience in a timely and powerful book about how you can break out of the crowd. Unlike giving you a formula to blindly apply, Ken gives you a proven framework to create your own route to success."

— **Atri Chatterjee**, CMO Zcaler,
former CMO Act-On and McAfee.

"Ken captures the essence of how to breakthrough in today's chaotic B2B markets. His battle-tested approach and insights will help marketing leaders think more clearly about establishing (and holding) a leadership position in their market."

—**Phil Lin**, former Director
of Product Marketing, FireEye

# LAUNCHING
# TO
# LEADING

*How B2B Market Leaders*
*Create Flashmobs,*
*Marshal Parades*
*and Ignite Movements*

## KEN RUTSKY

New York

# LAUNCHING TO LEADING
## *How B2B Market Leaders Create Flashmobs, Marshal Parades and Ignite Movements*

Published in New York, New York, by Morgan James Publishing. Morgan James and The Entrepreneurial Publisher are trademarks of Morgan James, LLC. www.MorganJamesPublishing.com

The Morgan James Speakers Group can bring authors to your live event. For more information or to book an event visit The Morgan James Speakers Group at www.TheMorganJamesSpeakersGroup.com.

## Shelfie

A **free** eBook edition is available
with the purchase of this print book.

ISBN 978-1-68350-034-6  paperback
ISBN 978-1-68350-035-3  eBook
ISBN 978-1-68350-036-0  hardcover
Library of Congress Control Number:
2016905701

**Back cover photo credit:**
Sandra Mahlmeister
©Wine and Jam Photography

CLEARLY PRINT YOUR NAME ABOVE IN UPPER CASE
**Instructions to claim your free eBook edition:**
1. Download the Shelfie app for Android or iOS
2. Write your name in **UPPER CASE** above
3. Use the Shelfie app to submit a photo
4. Download your eBook to any device

**with...**

In an effort to support local communities, raise awareness and funds, Morgan James Publishing donates a percentage of all book sales for the life of each book to

Habitat for Humanity Peninsula and Greater Williamsburg.

Get involved today! Visit
www.MorganJamesBuilds.com

# DEDICATION

*To Joel', Gigi, Mayson, Addie and Ochrutboo,*
*you are the best.*

*To Mom and Dad, I know you'll be proud.*

# TABLE OF CONTENTS

The Pre Game                                                          1
Preface                                                              3
How to Use this Book                                                 5
Introduction                                                        6
   *Game Film: The FireEye Story*                                   *11*

The Game Plan: From Launching to Leading                           15
   *Game Film: The Bear and The Alligator*                         *17*
Chapter 1   The Journey to Market Leadership
            and the Modern Marketing Machine                       20
Chapter 2   Why We Need a New Approach,
            The Changing B2B Market and Buyer                       27
Chapter 3   The Five Stages of Market Leadership                   37
   *Game Film: Velocity Football and You*                          *41*

The Opening Drive—Participation                                    45
Chapter 4   Unique Value, Creating Messages that Matter            47
   *The Coach's Corner: The Problems with Value*                   *52*
Chapter 5   Scaling Your Go-to-Market Messaging                     55
   *The Coach's Corner: Avoiding the YAWNER—*                      *62*
   *Why Most B2B Whitepapers Stink*

**The First Half Playbook—Breakthrough** **65**

Chapter 6    Introducing the Viewpoint Story Wheel    67
             *The Coach's Corner: Chasm, What Chasm?*    *70*
Chapter 7    Building Your Viewpoint Story Wheel    74
             *The Coach's Corner: On Approach, Innovation*    *82*
                *and Mindset*
             *Game Film: Viewpoint Sets*    *87*
                *the Stage at Cirque Du Soleil*
Chapter 8    The Four Viewpoint Story Types and    89
             Four Companies Telling Them Well
             *The Coach's Corner: The Hero's Journey*    *95*
Chapter 9    Which Viewpoint Stories are Right for You?    98
Chapter 10   Tilting to Abundance    102
             *Game Film: Palo Alto Networks Tilts the Playing Field*    *104*
             *The Coach's Corner: Scaling Your Viewpoint Story*    *105*

**The Second Half Playbook—Leadership** **109**

Chapter 11   Show Me, Don't Tell Me!    111
             *Game Film: Nimsoft Accelerates Sales Cycles*
                *with Online Demo*    *114*
             *Game Film: Dog Food and*
                *Stone Skipping—Something Quirky*    *115*
Chapter 12   Breakthrough Sales—Winning at the Coalface    118
Chapter 13   Breakthrough Marketing and The Modern Marketer    122

**The Final Drive: Winning the Champion's Cup—Transformation** **127**

Chapter 14   Beyond Breakthrough—Flashmobs, Parades    129
             and Movements
             *Game Film: DMTI Creates a Flashmob— From*    *133*
                *Key Customer Acquisition to Being Acquired*

*Game Film: GoodData Marshals a Parade—*     *136*
    *Messaging to Win in a Crowded Market*
*Game Film: Zuora Ignites a Movement—*     *140*
    *Transforming a Market*
Chapter 15     Market Leadership Uncorked—A Five-Step Plan     151

Appendix     Breakthrough Marketing Models and Frameworks     157
Acknowledgements     166
Sources and Notes     169
About the Author     173

# THE PRE GAME

# PREFACE

*We live in a challenging time for marketing and sales professionals in B2B markets. Information flows freely, markets are crowded, and buyers only engage on their terms, in their context, and on their timeline, not ours. Because of this, our old approaches don't work and we need to take new ones.*

*Buyers don't want to listen to us until that are ready to. To win, we must breakthrough a cacophony of noise and clutter and not only capture their attention but also powerfully communicate our unique value. But to lead our market, that's not enough. We also must tap into and exert influence over the context of the market conversation. Organizations that do this tilt the playing field to their advantage and become market leaders.*

*For the last 7 years as a consultant, and for nearly two decades before that in senior marketing operating roles, I've been helping to navigate these challenges and build market leading brands and businesses at Intel, Netscape, McAfee, and many others. I am super excited to be sharing my learning, experience, and new approach in this book.*

*Launching to Leading can help you breakthrough and lead your market by changing your stories, messages, and programs from me-too to unique, compelling, and breakthrough ones. When you do this, you embark on a journey that increases key metrics like leads to revenue by a magnitude or more. Winning examples from FireEye, Palo Alto Networks, Zuora, Virgin America and others are highlighted. The book also takes you to some interesting and unexpected places like Cirque de Soleil, Redmond Washington in 1995, and the world of Arkansas high school football.*

*I hope you enjoy reading this book as much as I have enjoyed creating it. I wish you success on your personal and professional journeys from Launching to Leading. May all your messages be unique, your stories be breakthrough, and your results be transformational. See you in the market!*

*Thanks for spending this time with me,*

*Ken Rutsky*

*Mountain View, California*

# HOW TO USE THIS BOOK

As a coach, referee and lifetime participant in team and individual sports, the "playbook" metaphor was a natural structure for organizing this book. You'll find it divided into The Game Plan, The Opening Drive, The First and Second Half Playbooks and the Final Drive.

There are three types of content within each of these sections—the main body of text, and two special types of content that add depth and color. The first special type is what I call Game Films, which are case studies and stories that directly or indirectly demonstrate or reinforce the content in the main body. The second are The Coach's Corners, which are commentaries that add additional explanation and theory to the practical.

Lastly, the appendix includes all of the important models used in the book. In addition, you will find a set of implementation templates and other tools online at kenrutsky.com. Please enjoy learning from my nearly 25 year journey in B2B marketing; I am excited to share it with you!

# INTRODUCTION

My first childhood was in the era of the cigarette, Chevy, Happy Days and the Partridge Family. It was the *"Mad Men"* era of marketing. Advertising was exploding; one day you were being told to "See the USA in your Chevrolet" and the next you were complaining, "I can't believe I ate the whole thing." Long-distance calls could bust a family's monthly budget, newspapers were king, and information was closely held and spun. Technology was a thing for technocrats; computers lived in big corporations surrounded by glass walls, and business-to-business marketing was limited to building brands, like General Electric's slogan, "We bring good things to life." In this era, when we didn't know the answer to something, we followed age-old advice: Go ask Dad. Even if he didn't know the answer, he often made it up, and yes, he probably still does. But now our children sit with their smart phones in hand while watching Netflix on their gaming system. When they have a question, they no longer ask Dad—they ask Google.

My professional childhood was spent in a world in flux. While working for the king of the old guard, IBM, I watched with both fear and excitement as information was beginning its long journey from datacenters to desktops, desktops to laptops, laptops to phones, and no doubt, one day, into our bodies. For every mainframe computer we sold at IBM, Digital Equipment Corporation and Wang Laboratories were selling dozens of mini computers. At the same time PageMaker and Lotus 1-2-3 were throwing gasoline on what had been a hobbyist market—the personal computer—and were about to change the entire world of information processing and sharing.

My professional adolescence started with me working for Intel. I saw the commoditization of compute power as Moore's Law relentlessly marched the Intel microprocessor line from the 386 to the 486 to the Pentium and beyond. It ended at Netscape with the advent of the graphical web browser, secure Internet transactions, JavaScript and more. When I left Netscape in 1999, Google had begun to emerge. "Go ask Dad" would soon be replaced with "Google it," and not just for kids—for everyone.

Now in 2016, we live in a world of information overload and commoditization where it's not too little information that confuses us, it's too much. The mobility of people, data and compute resources means that we are accessing data constantly, and the emergence of both businesses and social networks like LinkedIn and Facebook have changed the way we learn and validate information with our peers. On another front, companies like Amazon and Salesforce.com have led the evolution of cloud computing, forever changing the world of business computing.

In this new world, sales and marketing professionals must cope with the implications on communication strategies and tactics while at the same time the tools of their trade are rapidly becoming automated. As American entrepreneur, venture investor and Netscape founder Marc

Andreessen says, "Software is eating the world." And the world of sales and marketing is no exception; in fact, Gartner estimates that by 2017 the CMO will become the largest purchaser of IT software and services, surpassing the CIO. However, just because the tools change, the fundamental task of marketing teams stays the same: Create more and higher quality leads that lead to revenue growth. Or, as film-maker Spike Lee might sum it up, "Mo' Better Leads."

All B2B businesses need more and better sales leads, because leads fuel both revenue and customer growth. However, many organizations struggle with the trade-off between quality and quantity, efficiency and effectiveness. They invest heavily in marketing automation and content marketing only to find that they are generating a lot of leads, but the quality is poor. On the other hand, market leaders avoid this trade-off by being relevant in the market and capturing both more *and* better leads, efficiently and effectively. What market leaders have is great messaging and positioning to drive their content and automation investments.

With this backdrop in mind, it only makes sense to ask if some of our classic models of messaging, positioning and tactics need an overhaul. Are we still crossing the chasm, or has the world of instant communications obliterated its existence? Is the world of diagnostic solution sales and marketing still the most powerful approach, or do we need to transition to a more expert-driven, authoritative approach to the market? Does a vast library of product-marketing collateral really make a difference, or do we need to find new ways to communicate value to time-constrained and impatient buyers? Does our investment in marketing automation deliver if our content is still rooted in the old world of feature/function/benefit, or do we need to inform, inspire and teach with our content marketing efforts? And if so, what do we need to teach customers? Certainly not just about us, but also about how we can impact them in a strategically meaningful way.

To succeed, we must consistently deliver successful demand-generation and nurturing programs; however, successful demand-generation depends on a high volume of relevant and targeted content and not only that, but our content must punch through the crowded market to get noticed. We may know we are unique and valuable, yet we fail to convince enough people of this truth. Do we even know why we fail here? Even worse, the vast majority of our true competitive losses are not in the deals in which we compete, but in those we either don't know about or are too late to join.

At their core, markets are conversations between buyers and sellers about the exchange of value. B2B marketers who are stuck in the old world of feature/function/benefit fail to assert any control over the market conversation. When our value messages do not connect to the customer's context, they go unnoticed. However, when we do connect to the context of the customer's world, problems and opportunities, we can greatly influence the value conversation.

As we will see, B2B marketers who control the context of the market conversation have a disproportionate share of influencing how customers perceive value. Controlling the context of the market conversation is the key to driving both lead quantity and quality. Owning the market context puts us in more deals and at the front of the market parade, letting us lead the market forward and win more than our fair share.

Content is the fuel of any modern, marketing engine. We invest in people, tools and consultants to feed our growing needs for content and to power our demand generation and nurturing engines. The often-heard battle cry is: More content, more content, more content. However, content without context is low-test fuel, prone to knocks and stalls. Content in a powerful, customer-driven context—which we will call your Viewpoint—is high-test rocket fuel for you marketing engine, driving velocity up and to the right, resulting in dramatic gains in quality and quantity. As my kids might say, "Context rules! Content without context drools!"

This book will show you how to create a winning context for your brand by defining and telling your Viewpoint Story. Your Viewpoint is the well-planned and consistently articulated context that marries your value with the customer's reality taking them to a new more successful result. The Viewpoint sets the stage for your value discussion with customers and prospects. When done well, it creates a powerful, shared context for your market conversation that both resonates with *and* influences customers, tilting the playing field to the advantage of your unique value.

However, the sale doesn't end with attention. Today's buyers are impatient—they demand to see value early and often in the buying cycle. As many products have become more "service-like," demonstrating this value has become paramount. Gone are the days of lengthy Request for Proposals (RFPs) and drawn-out spreadsheet assessments of products. Products are evaluated, but services are experienced. Marketers must demonstrate the value of their solution across the entire buying cycle, through experience-driven communications and programs. They must scale their message into new channels, voices and segments. With aggressive scaling and experiential delivery, they can shorten and compress sales cycles, thereby increasing business velocity and achieving market leadership.

This book offers a powerful and proven set of methodologies to help you breakthrough and establish leadership in your market. Organizations adopting this approach—Breakthrough Marketing— don't just grow lead quality and quantity and increase deal velocity; they lead and transform their markets, growing market share and shareholder value in the process. I am looking forward to hearing and experiencing your brand's most important story. I hope you enjoy the journey with me to the front of your market parade.

# Game Film: The FireEye Story

In 2009, I had recently joined McAfee where I was running network-security marketing. At McAfee, we successfully grew the web security appliance business from about $60M to nearly $200M in a short, 18-month timeframe. We did this by defining and leading a new market segment that we called "Web2.0 Anti-Threat Solutions." Leveraging our unique capabilities married to our customers' self-identified challenges, we had repositioned away from the lucrative yet flat, Web-filtering market to something new and very valuable.

That success was squarely in the front of my mind when I met the FireEye team in late 2009. FireEye was then a small and innovative start-up with disruptive technology, a unique approach to network security and a handful of thrilled customers. The 2010 RSA tradeshow was looming six months away and the company wanted to re-launch and make a big splash. In order to understand this challenge, we need to do a bit of background on the network-security market.

At the time, there were two distinct market segments in network security: firewalls and intrusion prevention systems, better known as IPS. The firewall market was about a $4B market growing at 8–10% per year. The IPS market on the other hand was about $1B and not growing at all, maybe even shrinking. I was well aware of the dynamics of these two markets, having managed McAfee's go-to-market for both of these segments.

In addition to having dramatically different growth rates and sizes, the dynamics in the two markets could not have been more different. The firewall market was undergoing a major disruption from a start-up called Palo Alto Networks. We will look at their success later, but they had done what I would now call the classic "Better Mousetrap" Viewpoint and they were executing it nearly flawlessly.

Their go-to-market slogan was, "It's Time to Fix the Firewall." This worked great as the firewall market was primarily a replacement market. Customers were nearly mandated by compliance regulations to have them, and while they did function and deliver value, the incumbent products weren't simply unruly and difficult to use—they were broken!

On the other hand, the IPS market was in a state of consolidation and retrenchment. The penetration of IPS was much lower, and those customers who had invested in them struggled to get value out of the products. In addition, because these products were much more compute and bandwidth intensive than firewalls, they sold for nearly a magnitude more than their firewall equivalents.

When I arrived at FireEye, the team was considering trying to emulate Palo Alto Networks' success by positioning themselves as "Next Generation IPS." I raised three concerns with this positioning to the team. First, the market was shrinking and most of the revenue was in renewals, not new purchases. Second, the category was at risk of being subsumed by the firewall market, as firewall vendors were beginning to integrate basic IPS capabilities into their firewall. These reasons alone could argue against this strategy, but the third reason was by far the most compelling and powerful, and would be the launching point for FireEye's success.

Intrusion prevention systems were designed in the late 1990s and early 2000s to protect against existing network-security threats. Their primary mode of protection was the use of signatures; however, there was a nascent and growing belief—shared by FireEye's early customers—that signatures were no longer protecting organizations from the new types of malware-driven threats that were beginning to make the news. Based on this, and after some primary market research for both discovery and validation, we came up with this high-level story for FireEye's new positioning:

*The world has changed. Today's modern malware uses techniques and approaches that are far more sophisticated than anyone may realize. We have exposed this threat for what it is, and those responsible for network security need to address it head on.*

*If you depend on today's network security solutions made up of firewalls, web gateways and IPSs, which depend on signatures and other old techniques to protect you against this modern malware, the malware will evade your protection and you will be at an unacceptable risk of breach and loss.*

*What if you had a modern, malware protection solution that did not use signatures at all, but used a virtual detection engine, unique in the world, that was able to stop these modern threats by detecting them in action, while protecting you from breach and loss?*

At the RSA Conference in April 2009, FireEye launched their "Modern Malware Exposed" go-to-market messaging and initiative. We delivered an entire integrated go to market initiative around this message, complete with an e-book, a Web "micro-site" complete with diagnostic selling tools, demand generation programs, a full PR push and more.

This launch catalyzed a new, billion-dollar-plus market segment that eventually became known as Next Generation Threat Protection, with FireEye at the head of the charge.

Over the next few years, FireEye emerged as the leader of a market, grew its revenues into the many hundreds of millions, hired a high-profile CEO, and successfully executed an initial public offering (IPO) valuing the company in the billions of dollars.

● ● ● ● ● ● ● ● ●

When you finish this book, you will recognize the story above as an "All Pain, No Gain" Viewpoint, one of the four types of Viewpoint stories that can get you noticed, which is not a coincidence. While working for FireEye and replicating the techniques that worked at McAfee, I began to discover what are now the fundamental principles of Breakthrough Marketing. And as we will see, of all the components of Breakthrough Marketing, articulating a powerful context—or Viewpoint—for your messaging is the most important and impactful. FireEye's story is one of many examples we will review in this book.

In Launching to Leading, I have captured a playbook that lets you capture your brand's Viewpoint Story and create the messaging and positioning that will catalyze your market leadership. These tools build on my 20-plus years of participating in and observing B2B-technology markets. Since FireEye, I have used these tools to help companies win in their markets in not only security segments, but network management, price optimization, ice-machine rentals (yes, that's right), customer-success management, marketing automation, financial management and more. In this time, my clients have had acquisition or IPO liquidity events at a cumulative value of more than $6B with several others nearing or reaching "unicorn" status—a privately owned company valued at $1B or more. These tools have a unique way of finding the right answer to help you lead your market. FireEye is an example of a great success story, and I hope you can be the next.

The Game Plan
# FROM LAUNCHING TO LEADING

# Game Film: The Bear and The Alligator

*"In the battle between the bear and the alligator, the winner is determined by the terrain."*
—**Jim Barksdale**, CEO Netscape, 1995

On August 15, 1995, Microsoft launched Windows 95, its latest version of the dominant Windows operating system, with an over-the-top launch event on the Microsoft Redmond Campus. Broadcast live to theaters around the world, Jay Leno escorted CEO and Founder Bill Gates through the partner pavilion. Julie Herendeen and I were tucked in the corner of the exhibit hall, the Product and Channel Marketing Managers of a small piece of Windows 95 certified software called Netscape Navigator. Having reportedly failed to acquire Netscape a year earlier, Gates must have seen Netscape as a small but strong irritant—a thorn in The Bear's foot. Gates was soon to pen a famous email calling the Internet the biggest threat and opportunity in Microsoft's short but incredibly successful history. But today was a day to revel in the glory of the Microsoft world, and Gates wanted nothing to do with us. As Gates and Leno visited several partner booths, his handlers formed a virtual

17

wall in front of us, steering the cameras and microphones clearly away from our little corner of the pavilion.

The rest of the day was fairly uneventful for us; we entertained dozens of Microsoft employees, answering their questions about HTML tables, SSL encryption and what it's like to work at Netscape. All of them said "Cool!" and "Wow! Why can't Internet Explorer do that?" A few ominously added, "Oh, but we will do that soon with Internet Explorer."

A thousand miles south in Mountain View, California, scores of Netscape inside-sales reps rang customers to ask about their Windows 95 upgrade plans, using the event as an impedes to sell hundreds of thousands of Netscape Navigator licenses to anxious IT managers. Another team busily managed the shipment of boxes from Netscape's retail manufacturing partner through distributors and out to retail stores. Bundled with dial-up software, the boxed Netscape product would be the first on-ramp to the Internet for millions.

My email report back to the folks in Mountain View was pretty straightforward. It read, "Great reception of Navigator for Windows 95 from all attendees. Started several positive partner conversations with other third parties. Microsoft employees marveled at how far ahead Navigator is to IE. Everybody loves us, except Bill G., who did his very best to ignore and avoid us."

And despite our enthusiasm, we were clearly The Alligator, venturing into Microsoft's desktop forest. This was a frontal assault on the hegemony of Microsoft's empire. Had we made a mistake to stir the hornet's nest? Or was this a once-in-a-lifetime opportunity to create, lead and transform a market?

We had already created a mob scene around Netscape Navigator. We were selling Navigator in everything from packaged, retail dial-up software to ISP bundles to enterprise-wide site licenses. We were, as Geoffrey Moore said, "in the tornado" and the best we could do was to keep up with demand. Every mainstream news magazine—the ones that the Internet itself would marginalize over the next decades—called us the next Microsoft.

Our strategy was now to leverage the success of the Navigator browser to establish it beyond the desktop and make it the "universal client" for what we called the "Company Wide Web" but would eventually be called the "Intranet." Our mob scene was the browser, our parade was the Intranet, and our movement was nothing short of transformative for communications and commerce. With 25 years in retrospect, it is amazing how prescient this vision was. And while Netscape is now a distant marker in the business history of the Internet, the impact of the movement we started has lasted more than a generation. Being at a Netscape or a Salesforce.com doesn't happen to everyone, but it's a good example of a market leadership story to inspire us.

● ● ● ● ● ● ● ● ●

# CHAPTER 1

# THE JOURNEY TO MARKET LEADERSHIP AND THE MODERN MARKETING MACHINE

E veryone wants to be a market leader. Market leaders enjoy financial success, create wealth, and have recruiting, selling and market power that is almost always disproportionate to their actual product and solution advantages. In fact, many a competing executive has been driven crazy by this, lamenting on how their product was better but the market did not seem to care. These laggards launch new features continuously, believing that innovation will reverse this trend. They pour more money into demand-generation, expecting revenue increases to follow in proportion. They invest in better processes and pay higher commission rates, expecting volume and efficiency to improve. However, these efforts often don't pay off and they find themselves following rather than leading the market.

Yet some organizations do figure it out and become leaders. They position their products in the market and sell their value successfully. They tell their story powerfully and deliver a market-leading experience.

And this success has rewards beyond the qualitative goal of market leadership. Marketo, a leading provider of marketing automation software and a market leader in their own right, published metrics on leads-to-revenue-conversion percentages of its customers on this type of journey. Taking those numbers and extending them, the journey to market leadership looks like this:

## MARKET LEADERSHIP ACHIEVEMENT LADDER

| Focus | Market Leadership Stage | Leads To Revenue (number per 100 leads generated) |
|---|---|---|
| Experience | Leading | 5 |
| Viewpoint | Breaking Through | 3 |
| Value | Participating | 1 |
| Product | Launching | .5 |
| Concept | Hiding | 0 |

Figure 1: The Market Leadership Achievement Ladder

What then is going on? Why do some companies succeed and others fail to lead? Clearly no one wants to be a market follower, and at a first level most companies seem to be deploying strategies and tactics that look the same. Yet many get perpetually stuck in the launch and participation stages of the journey. Even those who receive rave technical reviews for their product often trail less well-reviewed solutions; their effectiveness never scales and they simply can't catch up. The leader to them looks like a snowball rolling downhill to success while they feel like they are pushing a boulder up a mountainside.

Fortunately, there is an answer to this question, and we will explore it in detail in this book. For now, let's postulate that leaders rise above product messaging and effectively communicate Value, drive context with Viewpoint, and deliver with Experience. But before we unpack that theory in depth, let's step back and take a quick look at the three core competencies at which market leaders excel. And by doing so, we will expose and explore the secret to their success and share a framework that, if followed, will help you climb this ladder, lead your market, and enjoy the financial rewards of that leadership.

## Building the Modern Marketing Racecar: Three Core Competencies

### Competency One: Marketing Technology—Build Your Engine

Modern marketers seem obsessed with marketing automation, and rightfully so. Advances in technology, analytics and advertising, and other related technologies means marketers have more power at their disposal than ever before. Scott Brinker, a leading market technologist who goes by the rather catchy moniker, the "ChiefMartec," tracks more than 3,000 solutions at the beck and call of marketers, up from less than 1,000 just a few years ago. Market leaders select and implement the right set of technologies to build the engine they need to succeed. Building a market leader without the right engine is like running a Formula One racecar with a lawnmower parts. The speed and agility needed to be effective and efficient simply requires deployment of the right technology.

Thought leaders like Scott—and others like my good friend and colleague Tom Grubb at Digital Pi—are masters at helping organizations navigate and select the right technologies to build their engines. While their approaches vary, they tend to agree on some basic principles. I've heard Tom articulate these several times to customers and they seem to boil down to these three simple guidelines:

1. Choose well-known, market-leading solutions, because the ecosystem will support you and you won't be re-inventing the wheel. You can find implementation help, best practices and a community of peers to help guide you toward success. A niche solution, even if 30% better, may take ten times longer to deploy, which you simply can't afford.

2. Resist the temptation to customize the solution. You will be tempted to customize and tweak the system—don't. As you scale, you will regret this. It will make your machine harder to extend with other technologies, slower to tune when needed and simply not as fast.

3. Add niche technologies and solutions, but do so cautiously. Although niche technologies are great, make sure they don't violate guideline #2 and that you aren't too dependent on them for success.

Market leaders follow this pattern and are excellent and successful implementers of marketing technologies.

### Competency Two: Content Marketing—Put on the Tires

For your marketing racecar to win, it needs great tires. Content marketing has emerged over the last decade as the best tires to put on that car. With the advent of the Internet, content became easier to create and consume. *The Cluetrain Manifesto*, an influential and forward-looking website declaration published in 1999, laid out the argument that "markets are conversations." Marketers soon realized that content was the key to participating in this conversation.

The Content Marketing Institute (CMI), an organizational thought leader in this space, defines content marketing as a "[…] strategic marketing approach focused on creating and distributing valuable, relevant, and consistent content […] ultimately to drive profitable customer action." Without content, the marketing machine can't roll. *Content Rules*, by Anne Hadley, is an excellent resource for building and scaling your content marketing efforts. Market leaders who build content marketing capabilities put the tires on their racecar and create efficiency in their marketing leadership efforts.

### Competency Three: Messaging and Positioning— Fueling the Machine

There's nothing new about marketers doing messaging and positioning; it's been a core competency for a long time. Great messaging and positioning is the fuel that drives relevance for your content marketing, creating an effective machine. Running on low-quality fuel leads to stalls, knocks and poor performance.

You may have guessed where I am going with this. CMI, in its September 2015 study titled, "B2B Content Marketing 2016— Benchmarks, Budgets and Trends," reported that the number-one challenge identified by content marketers was…drumroll please… "producing enough relevant and engaging content." But before we tackle why this is, let's summarize what our machine looks like with this simple diagram.

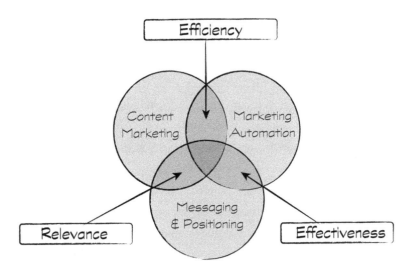

Figure 2: The Modern Marketing Racecar

To build a relevant, effective and efficient modern-marketing machine, we need to excel at marketing automation, content marketing *and* messaging and positioning. Time and time again, we find that market leaders do just that. They operate efficiently, publish a lot of relevant and meaningful content, and climb the ladder to Breakthrough and leadership.

### Stuck in Launch—Why We Stall

In client discussions I often hear about the need for more and better leads. When we dive into this discussion, we invariably end up chatting about all three of the machine's components: engine, tires and fuel. Although what I do typically hear from clients about messaging and positioning is that it's not as important as getting more content out.

Along with this, clients will propose strategies that involve more writing and technology. One prospect said to me, "What I really need is more blogs and videos." When asked what relevant content these blogs and videos would talk about she said, "I'll figure that out. I just need some videos or something."

When you have invested in the engine, it's *very* tempting to keep putting new tires on the car, hoping it will go faster. However, as we see from the Marketing Racecar diagram, being great at content marketing and marketing automation without great positioning and messaging may make us efficient, but it will never get us to relevancy and effectiveness. We *must* put the best fuel available into the machine. When I see organizations stuck in the launch or participation stages of this journey, despite great technology and gobs of content, I know that they need better messaging and positioning—they need high-test fuel for the machine.

Organizations failing to achieve market leadership that may be efficient but are "stuck in launch" must do a better job of messaging and positioning. That's clear; but how do you do that? That's what we will tackle next. To become a market leader—to lead your market parade—you must adopt the Breakthrough Marketing approach to messaging and positioning. Without this new approach, you risk the very real chance of being stuck in launch forever.

## CHAPTER 2

# WHY WE NEED A NEW APPROACH, THE CHANGING B2B MARKET AND BUYER

**M**ost CEOs, CFOs and VPs of sales have a jaded—if not skeptical—view of marketing. While they recognize the importance of marketing to their long-term success, they have a hard time understanding and measuring how well marketing is doing. Even in more mature organizations with a good handle on well-tuned marketing metrics and measurement, the question is still out there. With the advances in marketing automation, new channels of communication, and the avalanche of marketing data now available, marketing has evolved, in many CEOs' view, from a black art to a black science.

Hidden behind content marketing strategies, social media mysteries, and marketing automation dashboards and metrics lays a more fundamental problem. In today's hyper-competitive, global and instantaneous market, where buyers have nearly unlimited access to information and each other, the fight for their attention is like a crowded treadmill constantly gaining speed. With the proliferation of competitive solutions in even the most specialized market segments, and today's extremely well educated and self-directed buyers, we need a new marketing formula—one that delivers Breakthrough by combining Value, Viewpoint, engagement, experience and transformation. To do this, we must start by better relating our Value to the customer's reality, making our solution strategic to their success. Doing this requires us to create a new kind of message; one that tells our brand's most important story to the market—a story we call a Viewpoint. Before we dive into building our Viewpoint Story, let's step back and examine the three challenges we face today in getting Value noticed and winning in today's market.

### The Three Big Challenges to Getting Noticed and Winning

#### Challenge 1: Information overload

Without a doubt we live in a world of data and information overload. As anyone who uses Google knows, the challenge is not in finding an answer or result, but in finding the most relevant and meaningful answer. What does this mean for marketers? Let's examine a recent sampling of companies from the Andreessen Horowitz enterprise portfolio, shown in Figure 3.

Browsing the websites of each company allows us to determine its "market category," based solely on how each company describes itself. These terms are shown in Figure 4.

Finally, let's do an exact-term search in Google using the defined market-category names. Figure 5 shows the quantity of search results returned for each of these terms.

Figure 3: Sample of the Andreessen Horowitz Enterprise Portfolio

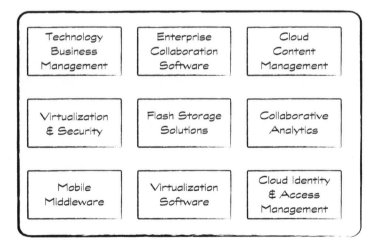

Figure 4: Self-descriptive Category Names

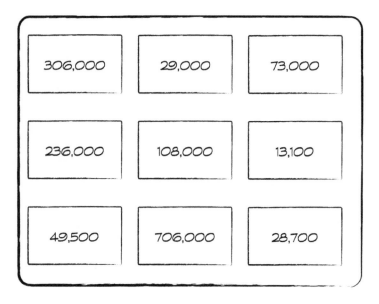

Figure 5: Results of exact-term search for each market category

It's clear from above and consistent with our intuition that there's a lot of noise out there. To make matters worse, users rarely use exact search terms, so this analysis tends to understate the true magnitude of noise in the market. Even in very niche market segments, we have hundreds of thousands of results returned for category descriptions. Rising above this noise is a tremendous challenge; it's like shouting to a bunch of teenagers wearing ear buds while a jumbo jet passes overhead. Breaking through this is a major challenge for today's marketers. It's no longer a struggle to get your information out there, but it's a battle to get it noticed.

### Challenge 2: Independent, connected buyers

Secondly, buyers are more connected than ever. A recent survey by CEB reported that 57% of the typical B2B sales cycle is complete before the buyer's first contact with vendors; before they've even met you, your customers are more than halfway through their decision process! They still get data from traditional sources such as analysts and industry publications but are now also connected with social media, peer networks and review sites. They get their updates in a short and constant stream of information, using always-on mobile devices to access social media, video and 140-character tweets. We've truly gone from a selling cycle to a buying cycle. More than ever, the buyer is in control.

### Challenge 3: Crowded Markets

In every category, markets are simply overwhelmed with competing solution providers. As we transition to a service economy, new entrants are leveraging technology and global labor markets, bringing new products and services to market that are faster, looking bigger than they are and aggressively filling market niches. Figure 6 shows just *one* market segment: marketing technology. This 2015 landscape graphic from Scott Brinker shows the logos of 1,876 vendors in 42 categories across six segments. And his 2016 version has over 3000 vendors. Imagine the challenges of breaking through to CMOs if you want to sell them something in this space! The CMO might make a dozen product purchases in a calendar year, so how do you even get notices let alone considered? This type of crowded market landscape repeats itself in virtually every buying center in the organization. In crowded markets, *every* product that gets considered has a positive ROI—that's "table stakes." Are you losing deals you aren't even in? Does your message go unnoticed? Are your competitors leading the market? Can't figure out why? The products that ultimately get purchased have a significant Return on Strategy, not just positive ROI.

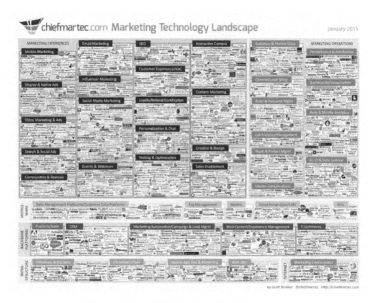

Figure 6: One of Many Crowded Markets—
The Marketing Technology Landscape

In the *Mad Men* era, these challenges didn't exist. All three of them are new consequences of the free-flow of information and lower costs of market entry enabled by the Internet and a hyper-connected world. The marketing world has changed, and there are huge implications for each of these changes. Summarizing these changes in a table looks like this:

| | Old World | New World | Implication |
|---|---|---|---|
| **Information** | Scarce | Abundant | From Search to Triage |
| **Buyers** | Dependent | Independent | From Sales Cycle to Buying Cycle |
| **Crowded Markets** | Few alternatives | Many alternatives | From ROI Hurdle to RO-Strategy Hurdle |

Table 1: Three Shifts in the World of B2B Sales and Marketing

In today's market, buyers are faced with an abundance of information and like many of us, they have more demands on their time than ever. In the old world, buyers depended on only a few, highly vetted and trusted information sources. Today, buyers cast a wider net, yet they must perform rapid triage on this information. Because buyers rarely engage directly with vendors early in the buying cycle, surviving this triage is critical to winning. In fact, those who Breakthrough early get the pole position in the race to the sale.

Due to the free-flow of information, buyers have become fiercely independent. In the old world, buyers were "managed" through a buying cycle by a professional sales rep. Today, buyers are running the show; it's become a buying process, not a selling one. Winning in a buying cycle requires a shift in both mindset and approach, as we will discuss next. Companies that continue to manage a "sales cycle" are playing yesterday's game.

Lastly, buyers are simply overwhelmed with great opportunities to invest in amazing products and services. Innovation shows no sign of slowing; in fact, it continues to accelerate. Traditional sales and marketing focuses on ROI; however, when faced with dozens of positive ROI opportunities, buyers must find a new way to prioritize investments. In order to win, companies must demonstrate strategic value.

This new world can be daunting for B2B sales and marketing executives and can wreak havoc with traditional communication and selling strategies and techniques. In today's world of information overload, buyer-centric behavior and crowded markets, information triage and return on strategy are driving buying priorities. To succeed, marketers must reimagine their approach to messaging and communication and change their entire mindset. Here's a simple recipe for what marketers should "AIM" to do:

- **A**pproach: *From bottom up to top down.* Rather than start with features, function and benefit, start with the customer's reality and world.
- **I**nnovation*: From benefit to Viewpoint and Value.* We must start with a well-articulated Viewpoint—an opinion about the world that aligns our value with the customer's reality, rather than shoehorning our reality and value into theirs.
- **M**indset*: That we must challenge and engage on the customer's terms.* Our job is to challenge the customer's assumptions and comfort. We have to move from diagnostic selling to authority-driven selling.

Proving ROI means nothing except a checked box. If you're not strategic, nobody notices; and if they notice, they just don't care. Yet, as we saw above, many organizations are still clinging to feature/benefit marketing and solution- and diagnostic-based selling. This worked well in a world with tightly controlled information, high barriers to entry and sales-led selling cycles. In today's reality, if you cling to those ways, you will be forever in the weeds of priority and importance.

Yet some vendors manage to rise above the rest, get noticed, grow and win far more than their fair share. As we will see later, companies as disparate as FireEye, Zuora, Virgin America and Salesforce.com have leveraged context to win. They do this by re-inventing their messaging and positioning to be top-down, viewpoint-driven and challenging. By doing so, they not only educate and engage, but they influence the way their customers see the world *and* how their solutions deliver meaningful, strategic value. They have mastered the art of telling their brand's most important story, their Viewpoint. Add a heavy dose of Experience Marketing into the mix and you reach Message Breakthrough and market leadership— you win!

Graphically, Figure 7 shows how our story comes together. Starting on the y-axis, we see that the markets for our products have changed, leading to what we see now; a buyer-controlled market where information is abundant, markets are crowded and buyers are independent. This contrasts to traditional B2B markets where information was scarce, competitors few, and buyers dependent on vendors and third-party experts for information. On the x-axis, we see the traditional go-to-market approach, based on feature, function, benefit, and managed demos. At the intersection in the upper-left quadrant, we see that if we take this approach, buyers don't care, notice or prioritize us. However, if we are able to change to the Breakthrough Marketing approach in the bottom right quadrant, one that is Viewpoint-based, Value-driven, and delivered with experience, we assert control and lead the market, our message breaks through

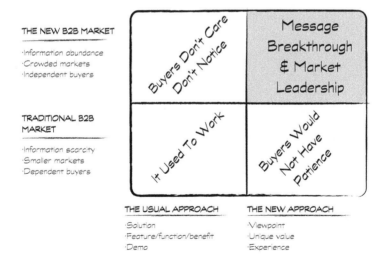

Figure 7: Why We Need a New Approach

and customers notice and prioritize us over competitors. We have succeeded in tilting the playing field to our advantage.

This "playbook" focuses on implementing Breakthrough Marketing, finding your unique Value, articulating a Viewpoint Story and scaling and delivering your message experientially. If you are still stuck in the left of this diagram, overly focused on feature/function/benefit and ROI and not articulating a unique, Value-driven Viewpoint Story, you won't lead your market. And in today's markets, leaders win and everyone else loses.

## CHAPTER 3

# THE FIVE STAGES OF MARKET LEADERSHIP

**A**s we have just seen, today's buyer is information overloaded, bandwidth constrained and fiercely independent. In addition, technology and the mobility of ideas, people and capital have lowered barriers to entry in just about all markets; meaning buyers are overwhelmed with attention and investment choices. Understanding these simple facts requires a radical rethinking of go-to-market strategies and tactics across sales and marketing. Those who react can see dramatic increases in marketing ROI and significant compression of sales pipelines, which can drop real dollars into the bottom line.

There are five stages of market leadership, depicted again in Figure 8. Each of these stages results in improvements in key sales and marketing metrics such as market-qualified and sales-qualified lead volumes (MQLs and SQLs), and pipeline conversion rates such as raw lead to MQL, MQL to SQL, and SQL to opportunity, and opportunity to revenue. In our ladder, we have chosen a key summary metric—the number of leads per hundred generated resulting in revenue—which is widely viewed as a good measure of overall marketing effectiveness. As you can see, climbing the Market Leadership Achievement Ladder can dramatically improve key metrics like leads to revenue as you grow market leadership and Breakthrough. The payback is enormous.

Let's take a brief look at each step of this ladder, and in doing so, preview the next three sections of this book.

### MARKET LEADERSHIP ACHIEVEMENT LADDER

| Focus | Market Leadership Stage | Leads To Revenue (number per 100 leads generated) |
|---|---|---|
| Experience | Leading | 5 |
| Viewpoint | Breaking Through | 3 |
| Value | Participating | 1 |
| Product | Launching | .5 |
| Concept | Hiding | 0 |

Figure 8: The Five Stages of Market Leadership

### Stage 1: Hiding—In the Lab

In this stage we are not "in the market" in any significant way. We are working with a small set of very early customers and tailoring our solution to meet their needs. Often, we may not even have a marketing or sales team. When we begin to prepare for launch, we engage in articulating the product features and benefits that matter to these early customers.

### Stage 2: Launching—Among the Many

When we launch, we focus on our product and making its presence known in the market. We try to magnify our early successes by positioning our product's benefits to our initial customers. Unfortunately, many organizations get stuck here because they are fighting a content-marketing battle based on features and benefits. In this stage, marketing effectiveness is dependent upon hitting buyers' needs with content that resonates with key benefits. But as most marketers are all too aware of these days, competitors are quickly commoditizing benefits. If it works for you, you can be sure they will copy it. Typically, we focus our messaging on our products and convert a very low percentage of leads to revenue; the quality of the engagement fails to inspire prospects to action.

### Stage 3: Participating—Focus on Unique Value

In this stage, the organization has moved beyond features and benefits and has articulated meaningful and unique customer Value. We are now messaging around value statements that have actual payback for customers *and* are unique to us and not as easily copied by the competition. Most organizations fail at even this simple task because they are so close to their product, enamored with its features and overly focused on style (coolness and feature differentiation) rather than substance. However, the reward to doing this well is enormous, with a 2–3x improvement in leads to revenue.

### Stage 4: Breaking Through—Aligning Viewpoint and Tilting the Market

In this stage, organizations have created a Viewpoint Story that converges on the biggest business changes impacting their customers and the most disruptive benefits that their solution delivers in response to those changes. They have aligned the customer value discussion with a Viewpoint that is a compelling and engaging articulation of the customer's worldview. They have set the terrain for the market conversation—tilting the playing field to their advantage. Organizations that achieve Value/Viewpoint alignment see significant improvement, often tripling their lead to revenue metric from the participation stage. Not only that, but they are growing both their market segment leadership and their reputation as trusted experts. IPOs have been enabled and billions of dollars can be made by effectively reaching and leveraging the leadership position that Breakthrough delivers.

### Stage 5: Leadership—Show Me, Don't Tell Me

Many marketers today are stuck in a world of whitepapers, videos and other explanatory content. When they do reach into engaging and experience-driven content, they do so as a "late in the sales cycle" component of their mix. This misses the fundamental need to satisfy the self-directed evaluation that buyers prefer today. In order to achieve velocity and capitalize on the opportunity from the Breakthrough stage, we must put experience front and center, early and often in the sales and marketing cycle. True leadership advantage happens when we have unique Value/Viewpoint alignment that's communicated in high velocity, engaging and experiential ways. This is a powerful position of market leadership that builds momentum and drives both revenue and shareholder returns dramatically upward. Organizations that reach this level of messaging and experience enjoy a nearly 10x lead-to-revenue advantage over those stuck at stage one.

 ## Game Film: Velocity Football and You

Before we walk through the ins and outs of achieving market leadership with Breakthrough Marketing, let's take a brief detour into the unlikely landscape of high-school football. Unless you're a hardcore American football fan, you have probably never heard of Coach Kevin Kelley of Pulaski Academy in Little Rock, Arkansas. His story is unique, inspiring and instructional. You see, Kelley's teams haven't punted since 2006. In a sport where it is not unusual to punt several times per game, Kelley has essentially kicked conventional wisdom to the curb. And those familiar with the game will recognize this as a radical departure from a strategy that has dominated the game for decades.

Here's a little of what Kelley had to say in a September 2009 Sports Illustrated article,

> *The average punt in high school nets you 30 yards, but we convert around half our fourth downs, so it doesn't make sense to give up the ball," Kelley says. "Besides, if your offense knows it has four downs instead of three, it totally changes the game. I don't believe in punting and really can't ever see doing it again.[...] Consider the most extreme scenario, say, fourth-and-long near your own end zone. According to Kelley's data (much of which came from a documentary he saw), when a team punts from that deep, the opponents will take possession inside the 40-yard line and will then score a touchdown 77% of the time. If they recover on downs inside the 10, they'll score a touchdown 92% of the time. "So [forsaking] a punt, you give your offense a chance to stay on the field. And if you*

*miss, the odds of the other team scoring only increase 15 percent. It's like someone said, '[Punting] is what you do on fourth down,' and everyone did it without asking why.*

Additionally, Kelley's teams onside kick on every kickoff, a tactic aimed at retaining possession and typically reserved for the most desperate of times late in a game when trailing. With literally dozens of variations of onside kicks, Kelley's opponents spend much of their preparation time learning to defend this tactic, forcing them to neglect other areas of game preparation.

To even casual football fans, this all sounds crazy, but you can't argue with success. Since deploying this strategy, Kelley has taken his small, 350-student school into the national, top-100 rankings and has captured five Arkansas state championships, all while winning over 90% of his games.

I refer to Kelley's brand of football as Velocity Football, not because it's a fast-paced game, but because of what we can learn from it in the context of Breakthrough Marketing. There are three big takeaways from this:

1. Kelley has established a unique Viewpoint. While conventional wisdom views football as a game of field position, Kelley says it's a game of ball possession.
2. Kelley then takes that Viewpoint and translates it into Value— in this case a strategy that says: Keep the ball in your hands at all costs.
3. Kelley then translates his Value and Viewpoint into a game Experience that delivers on the promise of possession. He is 110% committed to his worldview and he goes for it, despite naysayers and conventional wisdom.

Despite the overwhelming evidence and success of his strategy (he also onside kicks on every kickoff and lets opposing punts roll unfielded) and his growing popularity at coach clinics and the like, it is not apparent that Kelley has attracted many disciples. He's probably okay with that as he is amassing huge competitive advantage over his opponents. As the Sports Illustrated article continues:

> *Which is to say that most football coaches aren't simply averse to risk—no shock, there—but that they make choices at odds with statistical probability, akin to blackjack players standing on 11. The explanation: Subject as they are to scrutiny, coaches have incentive to err on the side of conservatism.*

This brings us full circle to Experience Marketing, a topic we will dive into in Chapter 11. While conventional B2B marketing wisdom is that only well-qualified and vetted buyers should see demos or receive trials, without fail in every scenario I have seen, the number one predictor of sales-cycle success is the presence of a trial, proof-of-concept (POC) or other real, hands-on experience.

Yet time and time again, sales and marketing teams that could easily move the trial or experience to the front of the marketing and sales cycle hang on to conventional wisdom, hiding or gating the actual product experience. Whether this is because of fear of failure, rejection of the new or concern about investors or CEOs second-guessing, those in the old world are punting away opportunity every day. Those in the new world—many of whom we will discuss in this book—are winning big every day, delighting customers and putting competitors on their heels.

Whether that means doing a try-and-buy, "freemium" model or live demonstration sites, you must put Experience front and center in your go-to-market strategy and tactics. It *will* give you the Kelley No-Punt Advantage.

It's no surprise that Kelley is out on the corporate-speaking circuit talking about thinking outside of the box. It's a simple recipe for winning: Look at the data; See it in a new way; Change your mindset; Have you got the courage to ask where else you can get a Kelley advantage? If you know, act now and win!

● ● ● ● ● ● ● ●

# THE OPENING DRIVE—
## PARTICIPATION

## CHAPTER 4

# UNIQUE VALUE, CREATING MESSAGES THAT MATTER

I n economic terms, Value is simply defined as the perceived benefit of a product or service net of its total cost. If we all understood how to effectively define and communicate Value, this book would be a lot shorter. Assessing Value is not as simple as we think, and many B2B companies get this wrong. It's all too easy to become obsessed with a product's features and benefits, failing to really engage the customer.

Communicating value in the world of B2B marketing is complicated by the following factors:

1. *Segmentation of customers and people within the customer organization creates different value by industry and role.* While at the top level we must articulate our unique Value, we need to be able to express it through a variety of "lenses" and "voices."

2. *Value is in the eye of the buyer, not the seller.* Value is articulated here as what customers are willing to pay for. It can be cool, but not valuable. Paying customers define the Value.

3. *Value is relative to competition.* We beat the competition by delivering more relative Value than the competitive alternatives, including the status quo. We must always put a competitive lens on Value.

4. *Value is subjective.* ROI is one measure of Value; however, there are many subjective measures as well that live in the buyer's mind. Without insight into the motivations, fears and aspirations of buyers (Viewpoint is a great tool to reach this insight), objective Value will often fail to deliver buyers.

Therefore, it's not enough to focus on Value generically; in order to win we must articulate *unique* Value:

*Unique Value = Total Value We Deliver—*
*Value Available from Alternatives*

Alternatives can be anything from do nothing, build your own, or buy from a competitor. But what about all those features and benefits and how do they play into our equation? Well, if Value is equal to benefits relative to cost, then unique Value must derive from unique benefits. Let's walk through the process of articulating unique Value.

The first step of finding unique Value is then to define those features and capabilities, focusing on the unique features or combinations of features we have. These unique features then drive a set of business benefits to our prospective customers. As depicted in Figure 9, the mapping can be one feature to many benefits, one feature to one benefit, or many features to one benefit.

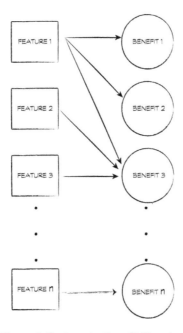

Figure 9: Feature-to-Benefit Mapping

However, customers *do not* buy features and capabilities, or even benefits; they buy the Value that is delivered by these. Without attention to this equation, marketers tend to be benefit- rather than Value-focused.

The next step is to ask which of these benefits are valuable to customers, meaning we need to evaluate these benefits based on customers' willingness to pay for them. Customers—especially technical buyers—might think a benefit is "cool," but if they won't pay for it, it's not valuable. Who knows what customers truly value? Typically we can ask our best sales folks and executives who are closest to paying customers to do this evaluation. We want to narrow our list of benefits to those that are truly valuable to customers. We will call this subset of our benefit statements our "Customer Value," as depicted in Figure 10.

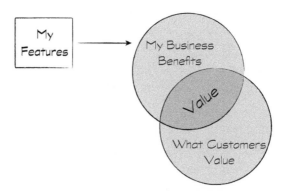

Figure 10: Business Value is the Intersection
Between Benefits and What Customers Value

However, we can often make the mistake of articulating a benefit in a way that causes the customer not to value it. In my work with dozens of clients in "Value workshops" we often reach a point where someone says, "But those are the benefits that everyone claims." My usual response is that in general, there are really only four benefits that B2B products provide: cost savings; increased revenues; productivity or efficiency gains; and reduced risk/improved compliance. Just about every benefit statement you can find is fundamentally a riff on one of these categories. Therefore the task is on us to articulate Value, not just benefit.

What turns benefits into Value, simply put, is that Value is benefits that customers will pay for. It is usually expressed in the what, how and why:

- **What**: Reduces sales-cycle by 5–6 weeks
- **How**: Shortens POC times by 60% (what took eight weeks now takes three)
- **Why**: So we can launch new revenue generating features faster.

This is how we move from a generic benefit (reducing the sales cycle) to a specific one (shortening POC times) to a substantial one (new revenue) by linking it to our features. So, Value statements go from *what* to *why* to *why us*? However, Value only is not enough; in fact, one of the biggest mistakes we make is to "overvalue Value."

This occurs when we are more excited about our Value than the customer is. In the above example, what if the long POC time is used by the customer to upsell their prospects? Then a shortened POC time might have a very significant reduction in revenues associated with it—not good! Or, the customer might love the value statement, but when it comes to priority, it is very low on the totem pole. This is why we must always ask, "will the customer pay us for that?" before we include it in our intersection labeled "Value."

Now we must ensure that our Value is unique to our ability to deliver. Because competitors can also articulate a similar equation, we must simulate that by honestly assessing the competitors' ability to deliver the items in the "Value" intersection. This changes the whole picture to something like Figure 11.

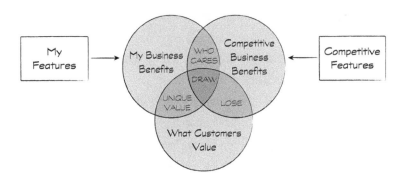

Figure 11: Unique Value Depicts the Subset of the Intersection of
My Business Benefits and Customer Value that Competitors Cannot Deliver

Simply put, unique Value is defined as the intersection of your unique capabilities expressed as business benefits, your customer's needs, and the missing benefits of your key competitors.

On this diagram, it's noteworthy that the "Lose" intersection represents things we either need to add to the product or minimize the impact in selling against. The "Draw" area is usually the "check box" features that all competitors have.

In summary, we first define our business benefits, then filter them against what customers value and what competitors can also do. This leaves us with our unique Value, which is then articulated in forms such as competitive positioning statements, messaging, market segmentations and product feature/benefit charts, examples of which can be found on kenrutsky.com

## The Coach's Corner: The Problems with Value

Value propositions and elevator pitches live in the rarefied air of marketing speak. They are almost seen as mystical accomplishments attained by only the anointed among us. Time and time we're asked, "but what's your elevator pitch?" Meaning, give me the 30-second attention grabber, or it's not worth my time.

While I agree that Value matters—and actually matters a lot—I think as sales and marketing professionals, we've worshiped at this altar for so long that we've lost sight of the end goal. We've become Value snobs. Here are my top five reasons why we overvalue Value:

1. *We are product narcissists.* Who doesn't love their own baby? Even when we clearly articulate customer benefit, we rarely ask if the benefit is truly valuable. We are often out of sync with

our customers' priorities, fears and aspirations. This might be the number one thing that drives great sales people to say, "The marketing guys are out of touch."

2. *Content is a commodity.* Whatever we write can be copy and pasted by our competitors with amazing speed, especially if it's good content. There are really only two benefits to products: cost savings and revenue increase; and there are only so many ways to say these things. Good content is not cheap or easy— for the first guy; but it sure is for the second! When we focus on the words that describe our Value, we lose to the second guy every time.

3. *If content is dead, context is the new king.* Value without context is like a tree falling in the forest with no one around to hear it. We spend so much time on Value we forget about Viewpoint. True Breakthrough happens when we paint our Value in the context of a Viewpoint that is aligned with our customers. We get away from our product obsession and set the terrain to communicate in a meaningful way.

4. *It all goes back to IBM.* Need Feature Advantage Reaction, Wilson Sales Strategy, Power selling… Most of what we do has its roots in decades old selling approaches. A world of technocrats who lived in glass houses could be sold to like that, but today's buyer is self directed, very smart and has access to more information than ever. Buyers have shifted the way they form opinions and make decisions from evaluation to experience and many of us have not kept up.

5. *Hard to experience = hard to use.* High-velocity sales require high-velocity Value delivery. Set the context and then "show me the money." If it's hard to demonstrate your value then your product or service must be hard to buy, deploy and get value from. The days of describing value are over; it's better to show

me 60% of the value in a compelling experience than describe 100% of it in a long document or video.

The real power of influence in sales and marketing has shifted from Content to Context, from Value to Viewpoint and from Evaluation to Experience. Don't lose sight of Value, but let's put it in its more appropriate role in our sales and marketing mix.

**X X X**

## Another Problem with Value

At the end of the day, there are really only four benefits our products can deliver: cost savings, revenue increases productivity and efficiency gains and compliance improvement/risk reduction. These are great, but the problem is, the buyer is overwhelmed with products and investments that have positive ROI and offer a compelling business case. To see just how overwhelming this can be, take another look at the Marketing Technology Landscape in Chapter 2. The bad news is that if you're selling to the CMO and his or her team, you not only compete with the products in your space, but with *every vendor* on this chart for priority and budget.

Business case is a must-have, but not enough on its own. The only way we win is to not only present a compelling business case by defining our Value well, but by raising the priority of our solution to the top tier—where they can be funded and executed. In order to do this we must be strategic, not just valuable. This is why context—or Viewpoint—is the critical first step in the market conversation. By creating a strategic context for our Value, we float to the top of the priority list. This is what I call Breakthrough—the second stage of the market leadership journey—where the combination of Viewpoint and unique Value is leveraged to influence customers and tilt the market in your favor.

## CHAPTER 5

# SCALING YOUR GO-TO-MARKET MESSAGING

**W**e've looked at how to build a strong and unique message. In the next section of the book, we will build a lead Viewpoint story to set the context for our unique message and Value. But how do we actually use it to get what we want and serve all the different purposes that it will be required for? In other words, how can we take our Viewpoint and Value story and messages and create dozens or even hundreds of pieces of content to fuel our content marketing and demand-generation programs with messages that will Breakthrough and build sales and market leadership? First let's introduce a simple concept called *scaling*. Scaling changes the perspective and depth of a story or message, making it highly effective for use in the communication and programs needed in B2B sales and marketing efforts. This allows for your message to be more quickly understood, believable and impactful along a wide variety of usages. To do this we will take a story or message and scale it down, up and out.

Scaling down is taking a long message like your four-act Viewpoint story (introduced in Chapter 6) and shortening it to its essence—think one paragraph or even one line. Scaling up would take that same four-act story and turn it into an e-book or even into four e-books, one for each chapter. Scaling out involves getting other experts to tell the story across many channels. Scale down for initial breakthrough; scale up for selling; and scale out for building programs and content deliverables. With the help of some superheroes, let's take a more in-depth look at each of these.

### Scaling Down: Ant-Man

I recently had the pleasure of watching the 2015 science fiction film *Ant-Man* with my wife and eight-year-old son. Given my height—5' 5" on a tall day—I am always happy when the little guy wins; it's a good message that the size of one's heart is what counts. Of course, it doesn't hurt to have a super-power suit that allows you to shrink from man to ant or anywhere in between. With maybe too much time to reflect on the movie I realized that *Ant-Man* held another secret—the power of scaling down.

How long does it take to tell the story of your company, product line, product or service? Have it nailed for the investor deck in three pages, or maybe in three paragraphs on the website? Maybe you even have it down to an elevator pitch in case of that infamous and hypothetical 90-second ride up the elevator with the CEO of a *huge* prospect. "So, what do you do?" he asks.

Answering this is no easy task for even the most seasoned business executive. She may be sure she has it down, but in the moment it may come out muddled, leaving her staring at the elevator buttons as she rides on alone. Even if she has something prepared that answers the three big questions that matter (Why buy anything? Why buy now? Why buy from me?), is that even good enough? In today's ultra-short-attention-span world, the answer is: probably not. Do we need to instead put on the Ant-Man suit, shrink down and hit small and hard? We do that on Twitter every time we tweet out of necessity, so why not our value proposition too? It turns out, shortening our Viewpoint story is the perfect way to do this.

Here's my answer to those three questions when I pitch CEOs my messaging methodology and service:

1. *Why do anything?* Information has become commoditized and B2B buyers are now fiercely independent and self managed; they don't want to hear from sales reps. The traditional feature/function/benefit messaging was built for an era of information scarcity.

2. *Why now?* If you don't change your approach, buyers in your market will get to short lists of vendors without you on them, and you will be losing deals you don't even know about! You will be stuck in launch forever.

3. *Why from me?* My approach is based on owning the context of the conversation before focusing on its content. Companies like FireEye, Palo Alto Networks, Salesforce.com and Zuora beat the competition because they created the market context and won. You can do the same thing with the Breakthrough Marking approach.

But the above is still pretty long-winded and complicated, so let's put on the Ant-Man suit and try again.

*To win today, you must reach buyers before they reach you. How? By creating and owning the context of the conversation to reach more short lists and win more competitive deals and move from launching to leading. I can show you how.*

But Ant-Man can still shrink at least one more time. *I can show you how to win by reaching more buyers and closing more deals by owning the market context.*

And ultimately this can shrink to just a tagline: *From Launching to Leading.*

We can all be long-winded, but to be successful we need to get comfortable in our Ant-Man suit, scaling down our messages to their core.

### Scaling Up: The Hulk

Now that we've talked about the need to scale down your go-to-market Viewpoint and messaging in the style of Ant-Man, let's utilize the Marvel Comics lineup and talk about scaling up—Hulk style.

You might be wondering why we're talking about scaling up when we just finished preaching the exact opposite? The truth is that in complex, considered purchases—which most B2B purchases are—buyers want details. They're looking for business, technical and reference details as well as data, data and more data. Scaling up is how we sell our product, service or idea.

However, scaling up your message has risks, and like the Hulk coming out of his street clothes, this can cause collateral damage— getting lost in the detail. Scaling up requires finesse and control, focus and purpose. We don't want to lose meaning by having it buried in too much detail. The purpose of scaling up is to give the audience greater understanding of your message by communicating it in a number of different ways.

There are four effective levers you can use to scale up: model, metaphor, examples and data. Thanks to Matt Church for teaching me this in his book The Thought Leader's Practice. First, for any message, adding a model can create a mental framework for the reader to put the value of the message in context and understand it better. For example, my model for scaling messaging is Down, Up and Out: Scale down for initial breakthrough; scale up for selling; and scale out for building programs and content deliverables. There you have it, a model.

Second, have a metaphor. In this case, scaling down is Ant-Man, scaling up is the Hulk, and, as you'll see next, scaling out is the Fantastic Four. Metaphors make messages stick and create emotional resonance with the viewer or reader. They allow an audience to quickly understand a new concept because it's delivered inside a familiar framework.

Lastly, I add depth to the concept with case studies and lots of data.

So now I've scaled my main message with both a model and a metaphor. Here's an example from Breakthrough Marketing: I've taken my story and message and scaled it *down* to tweets, *up* to blogs, e-books and this book, and *out* to workshops and speaking engagements.

The impact of a message depends on its ability to scale up. That's the trick to focusing the Hulk's energy; capture them with a scaled-down message and sell with purposeful scaling up. Ant-Man can get their attention but then you need the Hulk to knock down those buying doorways.

### Scaling Out: The Fantastic Four

Scaling out your messaging means having it Breakthrough and reach more people in more places. In today's modern-media environment we must package our messages with varied voices and deliver them across many channels. We must find the combinations of voices and channels that match the buyers we are trying to reach across different times in their buying journeys. Let's take a look at the two aspects of scaling out: voice and channel.

**Voice**—Because buyers naturally discount what any marketer or salesperson is telling them, the first dimension of scaling out is voice, meaning you need to find other voices to deliver your message. These can be grouped into three main categories: Experts, Influencers and Customers.

Experts can range from my CEO to a popular blogger working five layers down in customer support but who is an expert in an aspect of your business. Many people in the organization can now build social media followings and become known; tying our message to these experts is a powerful strategy to spread our message.

Influencers include journalist, external bloggers, analysts and celebrities, among others. Celebrities, of course, are not only pop-culture icons, but can be niche rock stars like Adrian Cockcroft (@andrianco) in DevOps or Bruce Schneier (@schneierblog) in IT security—they may not grace the cover of People magazine, but they have the celebrity of followings and influence in their markets.

Customers are, of course, the most powerful voice of all. When customers talk, prospects listen. This is true word-of-mouth marketing, where your own customers are the ones who draw in your next customers. Capturing your messages in the voices of customers is an investment where successful B2B marketers excel.

**Channel**—The second scale-out dimension is channel. Channels are where and how you scale your exposure. These can be split into two types: mine and others. In channels that are mine, I control spin, message, media and execution (e.g., my website, event, LinkedIn post, blog, e-book or on-demand online demo). For all of these, I'm the one designing, writing or commissioning them and I get to decide exactly how my messaging comes across. In channels that belong to others, I do not have full control because someone else is writing and deciding on the angle and the voice. But what I lose in control I gain in credibility. Whether it's a third-party website, event or news story, the gain in exposure and objectivity are what make "others" channels effective.

When we combine voice and channel we get the "Fantastic Four" of scale-out combinations. Simply broken down, they are:

1. Experts and influencers in *my* channels. Example: Third-party product review sponsored by me, downloaded from my website
2. Customers in *my* channels. Example: Case study video on my YouTube channel
3. Experts and Influencers in *others* channels. Example: Mention by analyst in tradeshow keynote
4. Customers in *others* channels. Example: Private reference discussion between customer and prospect

This is how a single piece of content can scale out in four unique directions.

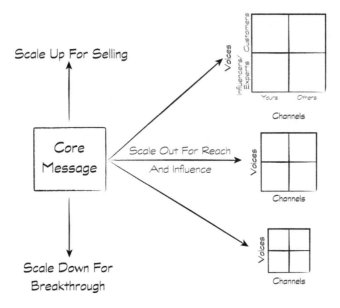

Figure 12: Message Scaling Roadmap

### Scaling Summary

Scale down like Ant-Man, scale up like the Hulk and scale out like the Fantastic Four. I've provided the individual pieces of a model for scaling your B2B message—down for Breakthrough, up for selling, and out for influence and reach. In summary, our model looks something like Figure 12 on the previous page.

# The Coach's Corner: Avoiding the YAWNER—Why Most B2B Whitepapers Stink

That's just a YAWNER—Yet Another White Paper Nobody Ever Reads. I contend that 98% of whitepapers from B2B companies are YAWNERs, both literally and metaphorically. Why is this? There are a variety of reasons, but they net out into three broad categories:

### 1) Ready. Fire. Aim.

First, as fundamental as it is, most whitepapers are simply not well targeted. Who is the audience? What is the current belief? What is the desired belief? What are the key messages? These are basic questions that any marketing professional should ask, but I am amazed at how rarely the product managers that I've spoken to or worked with can crisply articulate answers, even in retrospect. Getting sleepy yet?

### 2) The Kitchen Sink

Second, too many whitepapers are so long we've not only thrown in the towel, but the kitchen sink, too. Well, this is a great whitepaper about product X, so let's throw product Y into the mix because it's also strategic. Or let's try to make this serve "multiple audiences" so the business whitepaper ends up with five pages of dissertation on the ins and outs of our API set. You get the picture. If you can't cover a topic in ten pages or fewer, there's more than one topic. Break it up! If your targeting is on, the message should be lot tighter. Eyes drooping?

### 3) Get a Job!

Third, get a job! As much as we would like every project manager and product-marketing manager (PMM) to be a great writer, the fact remains that most are not. But a good editor (insourced or outsourced) can make all the difference. And PMMs out there who are reading this should insist on it. Take your knowledge and leverage it; don't try to be everything! Now *I'm* getting tired.

In summary, it's just plain simple:

### 1) Target

Make sure you have a clear view of who, what, when and why. Who is the target audience? What is the *one* thing the paper is teaching? When in the buying cycle do you want to deliver this to the target? Why should they read this and what is the new belief you'd like them to have once they're done?

### 2) Resist Scope and Subject Creep

Once you have the clarity on who, what, when and why, the keyword is focus, focus, focus. Resist the siren call of scope and subject creep. As long as we are teaching X, why not also teach Y? No—stop! Less is more. Stay focused and the length and depth will be right to suit your marketing and communication objectives. Pick a topic and stick with it: one message, one goal and one call to action. Use the creative brief for a focusing tool and exercise before you start writing. There are few whitepapers that should be longer than 10–15 pages. If you have 20 pages, consider if there are really two papers that can each stand-alone but also work as a series.

### 3) Get the Right Skills Deployed

Find the team. Don't outsource your domain expertise, but the right designers, editors and even writers should be deployed. Be honest about your team's writing skills and supplement them as needed. Don't skimp! It's better to spend a bit more time and money to get a product that is readable and meets your objectives than to deliver a low-quality YAWNER.

My estimate is that about 2% of whitepapers are actually readable, powerful marketing tools. Most are poorly targeted, unfocused, poorly executed or a combination of these. This makes them unsuccessful. But good targeting, consistent focus and quality execution is the recipe for making your investment stand out and deliver results.

**X X X**

# THE FIRST HALF PLAYBOOK— BREAKTHROUGH

## CHAPTER 6
# INTRODUCING THE VIEWPOINT STORY WHEEL

Viewpoint is the first and most important element of moving from participating to Breakthrough and beyond in the Market Leadership journey. Our Viewpoint is the *context* for all of our Value-based messaging. If we can articulate a context that is meaningful to the customer and in sync with our Value delivery, we can tilt the market to our advantage. This is the goal of the Breakthrough leg of our journey.

How then do we create a powerful Viewpoint? A Viewpoint can simply be thought of as the story you tell that explains why you are bringing your product or service to market. It is a story with four acts that go like this:

Act 1: One or more things in your world have changed and left you in today's new reality.

Act 2: If you depend on the expected solutions X and Y, which were built for the old reality, you will be left with unmet needs and/or missed opportunities.

Act 3: What if you had an unexpected approach to X that was a re-imagined solution for today's reality that looked like this.

Act 4: Then you would end up in a transformed future state where you would solve problems and capture opportunities in today's new reality.

And in reality, each of these acts can be its own individual story while also contributing to the complete Viewpoint story, which we will focus on now. Graphically, we can depict this as a "story wheel" as shown in Figure 13.

THE VIEWPOINT STORY WHEEL

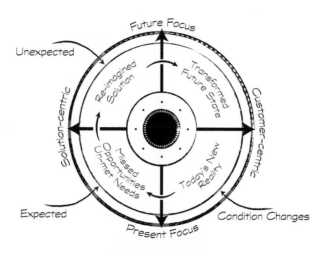

Figure 13: The Viewpoint Story Wheel

By filling out this story wheel from the bottom left and moving clockwise, you can create a powerful and meaningful Viewpoint story palate. The story wheel for this book's Viewpoint is shown here in Figure 14.

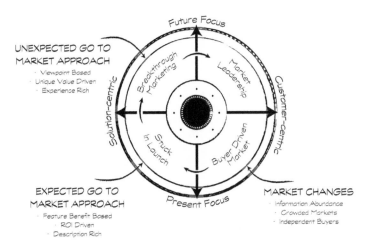

Figure 14: This Book's Viewpoint Story Wheel

We can read this story wheel using the four-act structure above and we have this story template:

## Act 1: The Buyer-Controlled Market
In today's crowded B2B Markets, information is abundant and buyers are independent, creating a new reality of the buyer driven market.

## Act 2: Buyer's Don't Notice or Care
If you depend on the expected market approaches of feature/function/benefit and descriptive, ROI-based selling (both of which were built for

the old reality of vendor-managed solution selling), buyers won't notice you and won't care.

### Act 3: Breakthrough Marketing, A New Approach

If you took a Breakthrough Marketing approach that focuses on your Viewpoint and Unique Value, and deliver it with experience over description…

### Act 4: Message Breakthrough and Market Leadership

…then you would end up with exceptional messaging Breakthrough, thus establishing market leadership and winning more deals because you have aligned your Value with the buyer's reality, pain and opportunity.

Of course, this is merely a short summary of this story, but one that encapsulates the entire value of Breakthrough Marketing in an impactful way. In addition, this story is balanced across the four parts of the wheel and as we will soon see, an effective Viewpoint can be weighted in any of the four quadrants. In fact, we have many stories to tell from this single palette.

In the next two chapters we will discuss how to build a Viewpoint Story Wheel in a step-by-step process and we will look at the four types of stories we can build from that wheel. We will also explore examples of each and provide guidance for picking the right Viewpoint story to lead with, and how to scale your go-to-market, top-of-funnel messaging with a broad palette of Viewpoint stories.

# The Coach's Corner: Chasm, What Chasm?

B2B sales and marketing used to be about the classic Influence Pyramid and in technology marketing, Geoffrey Moore's *Crossing the Chasm* was the defining marketing paradigm. However, the world has changed since 1991. Influence is now fluid as opposed to structured, and arguably the classic adoption chasm has collapsed. There are three interrelated trends driving this collapse. None of these in and of themselves will surprise you, but when taken together, there is a compelling argument that the chasm is collapsing. Smart marketers can speed time to adoption by understanding this dynamic.

These trends are:

- The consumerization of technology and its impact on the speed of diffusion
- The commoditization of the creation and distribution of content
- The lower barriers and risks of technology solution adoption

*Crossing the Chasm* might be the most dog-eared book in any marketing library. It is a classic that has guided much marketing thought and practice over the last two decades and still has tremendous teaching and learning value

But today we need to take a hard look at the chasm; does it really still exist? Hasn't the market dynamic changed? On page xi of Moore's revised, 1999 edition he writes:

*The Chasm Model itself represents a pattern in market development that is based on the tendency of pragmatic people to adopt new technology when they see other people like them doing the same. This causes them to band together as a group, and the group's initial reaction, like teenagers at a junior high dance, is to hesitate and watch.*

Let's dissect this very statement of the Chasm Model.

1. *"[...] the tendency of pragmatic people to adopt new technology when they see other people like them doing the same."* Since the Chasm was "discovered" by Moore, technology has infiltrated our lives. As Marc Andreessen says, "Software is eating the world." Early adopters are everywhere and kids and consumers often lead the way. In addition, technology continues to be hidden behind a better and easier user experience. Today's professionals are more comfortable with and better and faster adopters of technology. From the secretary to the CEO and the line worker to the general manager, adoption patterns have compressed and changed. CIOs and business managers who wait for the mainstream to adopt a solution will quickly find themselves in the late majority, falling behind competitors.

2. *"This causes them to band together as a group [...]"* Which group? How many affiliations do you have on LinkedIn and to how many communities do you belong? It used to be that vendors held the information and customers and buyers depended on information brokers such as Gartner, IDC and others to get aggregated views of it. Now they can go to Quora, LinkedIn or Google. Vendors now invest fortunes in content creation and distribution because they must inform buyers now or lose to competitors who do. The group of peers has expanded dramatically and the information available to these groups has become free, available and subject to peer review. One of the main reasons the group effect put brakes on mainstream adoption was the difficulty of obtaining and evaluating vendor claims. We've entered the era of transparency and visibility, where the early adopters can more effectively share and make their informed views and experiences real to the mainstream.

3. *"[...] and the group's initial reaction, like teenagers at a junior high dance, is to hesitate and watch."* The new reaction is to

try, at a small scale, to fail and scale successes. The speed and cost dynamics of the cloud have fundamentally changed the economics of trial and the risk of failure. The risk and fear of failure is now lower than the odds of success and upside.

Like the coaches who continue to punt, most marketers continue to use the same playbook with mediocre results while others are winning around them. In a chasm-less, information rich and hyper-connected world, the first challenge that marketers face is getting noticed. Buyers don't care about features, benefits or even value when it is not presented in the context of their reality. Buyers rule and if sellers want to get their attention, they must articulate a compelling, unique and aligned Viewpoint with their customer.

## CHAPTER 7

# BUILDING YOUR VIEWPOINT STORY WHEEL

**B**uilding a comprehensive Viewpoint Story Wheel is the first step to telling your most compelling story—your Viewpoint. Prior to walking through this exercise, you may feel confident in your current articulations of a Viewpoint, whether explicit or implicit. In this case, the process of completing the Viewpoint Story Wheel can lead to an increased depth and elegance to your story and you will likely discover new insight along the way. If coming up with your Viewpoint has so far felt confusing and overwhelming, then this process will make the completion both doable and powerful. We simply start from the bottom right of the story wheel and work our way clockwise to the upper right. Building your Viewpoint Story Wheel is a four-stage process:

Stage 1: STEEP into the customer's new reality

Stage 2: Build the pain/gain gap

Stage 3: AIM to a new solution

Stage 4: Define the future state

### *Viewpoint Story Wheel Stage 1:*
### *STEEP into the Customer's New Reality*

Most business people are well aware of the SWOT analysis framework to assess the Strengths, Weaknesses, Opportunities and Threats of a company, product or strategy. However, far fewer have heard of STEEP. STEEP—which stands for Social, Technological, Economic, Environmental and Political—is an excellent tool used to scan an environment in order to understand it.

Most solution providers will focus on only one of the STEEP factors when they think about their customer's world. Bankers think about economics; environmental consultants think about environment; technology providers think about—you guessed it—technology. This myopic view of the customer's reality is self-serving and self-defeating. We need to do better. STEEP is an excellent tool to help open our eyes and find trends that we might otherwise miss, forcing us to step outside our world and specialization into a more holistic and powerful view of the customer's reality.

STEEP may seem complicated, but it's actually simple if you follow these five straightforward steps:

**Step a**: We gather our customer experts and even some friendly customers and brainstorm a list of the top 3–4 issues or opportunities facing the customer in each of the STEEP areas.

**Step b**: We rank them in order of importance to the customer. We define importance as the degree to which the item matters to either risk or opportunity to the overall business.

**Step c**: Once we have identified the top 10 factors we rank order them into the top five that our solution can positively impact, such as E: Segment specialization; P: Increased privacy regulation; and T: Mobile device proliferation among customers.

**Step d**: We then define the old reality as the opposite set of points so we can make statements like, E: *"It used to be that our customer's industry players were one-stop providers of broad solutions but there is a big move from consolidation to segment specialization."*; P: *"We are under ever-increasing regulatory scrutiny over privacy of customer information where we need to change from our standard of care and process oversight."*; and T: *"Our customers are demanding self-service support and renewals on mobile devices."*

**Step e**: We then combine these statements to form a new-reality label. For example, Zuora added a compelling set of economic, technology and business trends together and labeled them "The Subscription Economy," described the on their website like this:

> *Commerce has evolved. In the last 10 years, there's been a dramatic shift in the way both consumers and companies want to do business. Today, people would rather subscribe to services than buy products. It's happening everywhere. And it will have a dramatic effect on your business.*

STEEP is an exercise that can pay off in many ways because it helps create a powerful picture of the reality facing your customers today. You can then genuinely engage with them by showing a deeper and more nuanced understanding of their world, framing your value conversation in their context, not yours.

### Viewpoint Story Wheel Stage 2: Building the Pain/Gain Gap

By articulating the customer's unmet needs and missed opportunities we define the need for our solution in the context of the customer's reality. In other words, given the changes to their reality that we have highlighted in Viewpoint Story Wheel Stage 1, we then answer this question:

*Given the products, solutions or processes the customer has traditionally used to solve the problems that our solution addresses, and given the changes in the new reality, what are the unmet needs they can't solve and the missed opportunities they are experiencing?*

Building the Pain/Gain Gap is done with the same group of customer experts from STEEP Stage 1, especially those with regular customer interaction. We build the Pain/Gain gap by following these four steps:

**Step a**: Articulate the approach and products that customers use to solve problems in our category today. *Example: Today's network security solutions are signature based.*

**Step b**: For each of the key trends identified in Step 1, list the shortcomings of the current approaches to solve this problem. *Example: The new reality is that attackers and attacks have changed and they are largely able to evade signatures.*

**Step c**: Define the consequence of this shortcoming. *Example: So if you are depending on signatures, you will suffer losses at the hands of these new attacks.*

**Step d**: Add these statements together to define the Pain/Gain Gap label. *Example: Modern Malware Risk*

You are now ready to tackle the third step of your Viewpoint Story Wheel creation—AIM to a New Solution.

### Viewpoint Story Wheel Stage 3: AIM to A New Solution

It might seem trivial and simple to express what is re-imagined and unexpected about our product or service. In fact, that's why we love our product. Some of the best products in the world were built by people who had a problem with the current reality and could not solve it with the usual solutions available; so they built a better mousetrap and then said, "Hey, if I could use this, I bet a lot of people could." The problem is, they tend to sound like this...

> *When I worked at Acme, we were faced with a situation where our protocol for X was incompatible with our current business solutions. What we really needed was a feature that we call FOO that integrates the existing infrastructure with the emerging need for cross-channel communication and is compatible with.... That's why we built this new Dweelybopper.*

...when they need to sound more like this:

> *When I worked at Acme, we were faced with growing margin pressure, increased regulatory scrutiny and a process for Y that was not responsive and was too costly. Not only that, it was totally isolated from our current process, leaving us with unsustainable cost and compliance trade-off. What we really needed was a new approach that was driven by people, not technology, and started with a whole new mindset that we could increase compliance AND reduce cost. Once we understood that, we knew if we only had an innovation like FOO that allowed us to.... That's why we built this new Dweelybopper.*

Notice the subtle difference? We are not just telling the *what*: the FOO-enabled Dweelybopper. Based on our STEEP analysis, we have been much more explicit about the *why*: leaving us with unsustainable cost and compliance trade-off. And most importantly we are not just focused on one, but three *hows*:

- Approach: *People, not technology driven*
- Innovation: *The FOO*
- Mindset: *That we could increase compliance and reduce cost*

By crisply articulating the Approach, Innovation and Mindset, we not only create a context for our innovation, but we make it *dramatically deeper and more compelling and interesting*—exactly what we AIM to do!

We can think of this in a simple triangle framework shown here in 15:

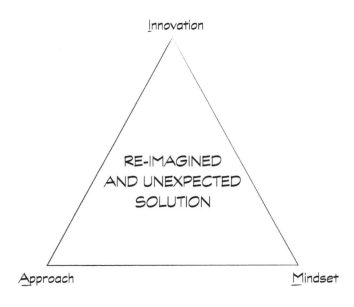

Figure 15: The AIM Solution Framework

By casting our innovation in multiple dimensions, we bring it to life, add memorability and create Breakthrough. Our innovation is no different, but by spending the time talking about our approach and mindset, more and more people will care and remember.

*Viewpoint Story Wheel Stage 4:*
*Define the Transformed Future State*

What's the unexpected new world you will take your customer to? This transformed future state is the climax of our Viewpoint Story Wheel. It sits opposite the unmet needs and missed opportunities segment of the wheel and articulates the benefit and advantages of the entire journey you have taken the customer on. Your group of experts should now:

- Define the new "state" that customers are in after they successfully adopt and implement the re-imagined solution defined in Stage 3.
- Describe this new state in a series of statement such as:
  o The benefit of taking advantage of previously missed opportunities.
  o The peace of mind resulting from solving previously unmet needs.
  o The leadership position they are now in; what is the parade your customer is now leading?
- Label this spot on the story wheel

Our detailed version of the Viewpoint Story Wheel now looks like Figure 16 on the next page.

Completing this wheel enables us to write our Viewpoint story in its generic-form, four-act structure repeated here:

**Act 1**: One or more things in your world have changed and left you in today's new reality.

**Act 2**: If you depend on the expected solutions X and Y, which were built for the old reality, you will be left with unmet needs and/or missed opportunities.

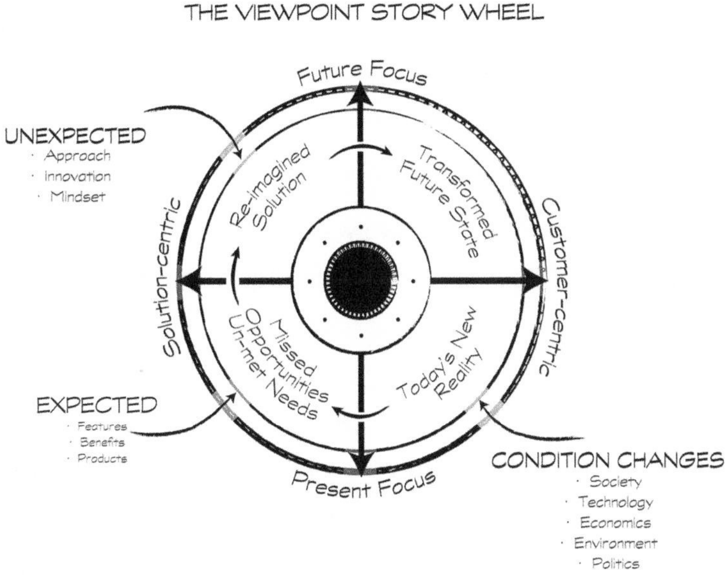

THE VIEWPOINT STORY WHEEL

Figure 16: The Detailed Viewpoint Story Wheel

**Act 3**: What if you had an unexpected approach to X that was a re-imagined solution for today's reality and looked and was built with this approach, innovation and mindset?

**Act 4**: Then you would end up in a transformed future state where you would solve problems and capture opportunities in today's new reality.

However, as we will see in Chapter 8, there are actually four types of Viewpoint stories we can spin from the story wheel, all depending on our choice of both present/future and customer/solution filters. I call these four stories *Trendspotting*, *All Pain/No Gain*, *Better Mousetrap* and *Brave New World*. Each of them puts a bigger emphasis on one Act (or quadrant) of the story wheel. After reviewing these story types in Chapter 8, Chapter 9 will provide guidance for choosing the story type that is the right lead or focus story for you and your market. Once we choose a focus, we then can tell short stories based on each of the other quadrants of the story wheel as part of our scaling strategy, which we will cover in Chapter 10.

# The Coach's Corner:
# On Approach, Innovation and Mindset

**Approach** is most often overlooked in the articulation of our re-imagined solution. One well-known, simple example is plenty to show the power. Salesforce.com said their approach was the "End of Software." In some ways this is pure bunk. Surely, the Salesforce service is built with software. In fact, the very description of services like this is now known as Software as a Service (SaaS). What founder Marc Benioff really meant was expressed here "Our approach is that our customers should not have to deploy, manage or maintain CRM software on their own servers or datacenter; we will deliver the value of CRM hosting the software for them." This proved to be a critical distinction for Salesforce.com to build its empire. This seems obvious now, but at the time it was a revolutionary approach to value delivery in the enterprise business software market.

In general, there are three areas of approach innovation. They are Methodology, Go-to-Market and Value Delivery.

- Methodology is a set of processes and practices we use to solve a problem. Innovations in methodology include things like crowdsourcing, agile development and content marketing. Methodology innovations usually require technology innovation and business-model innovation to support them.

- Go-to-Market innovation involves changing the way products are sold, distributed and/or promoted.
- Value Delivery innovation involves changing how or what value is delivered to the customer. For example, the biggest innovation in Google's core search business was arguably not their world-class indexing and search capability, but the AdWords program. Prior to Google AdWords, advertisers on search sites primarily bought directory or channel-based banner ads sold on a pay-per-impression basis. Google changed the search advertising paradigm by dramatically increasing the value delivered to the advertiser by allow them to display content-based ads tied directly to the keyword searched. This resulted in a magnitude level improvement for search advertisers and built the Google business revenue machine. Almost all of the search-technology innovations that followed were both enabled by and in service of this value-delivery innovation. Value-delivery innovation involves changing or creating new ways to capture and deliver value. For example, OpenDNS, a network security service provider, innovated in their business model by crowdsourcing their data by giving away service to consumers. By establishing a huge consumer-install base, OpenDNS got visibility into a huge percentage of Internet traffic and mined that data to create valuable, for-fee B2B services from the dataset.

**Innovation**—Despite the fact that we live in a technology-driven world, innovation can still come in other forms. Business model and packaging also offer ways to innovate.

Business-model innovation usually involves changing the structure of the generally accepted business model in an industry. This could be eliminating or disintermediating a member of the value chain or changing the way a product is priced, such as from purchase to subscription. The Subscription Economy is a macro-level business model innovation discussed in this book. eBay changed the world of collectibles by opening a new sales channel to collectors of online auctions, removing barriers of time and space that existed with flea markets, and in-person auctions and garage sales that were the traditional channels for many person-to-person sales.

Packaging innovations can often change markets. By combining functions we can change purchase preferences and behavior. The iPhone's initial success was largely due to the combination of music player and phone, delivering incredible value to consumers who preferred not to carry both devices. Fortinet built a business by delivering their Unified Threat Management (UTM) appliance, delivering Firewall, IPS and Mail and Web Gateways—previously four different products—to small and medium businesses where space and management bandwidth are at a premium.

In most cases of mindset, approach and business-model and packaging innovation, a set of technology innovations are needed to support and deliver their value. Without Google's technology enabling them to build and maintain an accurate and blazingly fast index of the Internet, AdWords would never have exploded. However, technology innovation is often meaningless outside of the context of business model, approach and mindset. A big mistake many B2B technology companies make is to focus solely on their "really cool" technology innovations and lose the context and surrounding value that they aspire to deliver to paying customers.

**Mindset**—I initially began working on Mindset in 2006 when I explored the SaaS Mindset as being composed of three-dimensions orientation, perspective, and focus.

Since then, Mindset has come up in my work with technology clients, not only in the SaaS context but also in the discussion of transformative selling. It was present again in my nonprofit work with our local school district and lastly in some work I've started on career transitioning from engineering to marketing. In all cases, my Mindset framework has proven to be a quick and powerful way to both explain and leverage mindset as a way to understand and drive transformations in belief and action.

The Mindset Framework:

Mindset is made up of three components: Orientation, Perspective and Focus. In the framework, each of these has a very specific definition.

1. Orientation: My relationship and adjustment to the environment that I am in
2. Perspective: My way of regarding/judging and interpreting facts
3. Focus: Where I choose to concentrate my attention

Let's take a look at a couple of examples.

### Example #1: The SaaS Mindset

Because SaaS is a very different business model than licensed software, SaaS providers—most of who came from the licensed-software world—needed to change their mindset as follows:

- Orientation from Product to Service
- Perspective from Spiky to Continuous
- Focus from Transactional to Relationship

Without these changes, the incentive to drive the organizational requirements for success and the framework to make strategic choices would be flawed. I saw many cases where ISVs have not succeeded with the transition to SaaS, not because of technical barriers, but because they failed to change their mindset and therefore made poor organizational, resource and strategic choices.

### Example #2: Transitioning an educational institution

There has been a lot of talk in our schools about the pressure put on young students to perform to ever increasing academic standards. Tales of parents worrying about whether their preschool is the right feeder to the Ivy League is now a cultural meme. Fighting this are documentaries like *Race to Nowhere* and *Waiting for Superman*, which document the huge costs to our children and society of this overemphasis on achievement. Locally, I've been working with our elementary school on trying to raise "whole children" and what this means to the community. I believe that to succeed we must redefine the mindset when it comes to the community's goals for public schools.

- Orientation: From Curriculum to Learning
- Perspective: From Achievement to Development
- Focus: From "Teach to the Test" to "Teach for Life"

I firmly believe that if we can shift our mindset regarding educational goals, we can not only raise healthier, happier children, but can actually improve our levels of achievement.

### Example #3: Transitioning careers from engineering to marketing

I work with a lot of engineers, many who have marketing in their job titles. The number one thing separating those who successfully make this transition from those who don't is a change in mindset.

- Orientation: From Technology to Business
- Perspective: From Details to Big Picture
- Focus: From Problem Solving to Solution Sharing

Engineers who fail to change their mindset are easy to spot. They have a hard time focusing on scale-related business problems and solutions. They get trapped in features and functions and can't see the proverbial forest for the trees.

As you can see from above, the Mindset framework can be applied to a wide set of transformations, from organization to cultural to individual. So the next time you are faced with a transformation that is failing or struggling, step back and examine the orientation, perspective and focus that you, your organization or team has adopted, and analyze whether it's the right one for success or is anchored in your behaviors and beliefs of the past.

When applied to Viewpoint and AIM, Mindset describes how you have changed the way you solve your customers' problems from this perspective.

**X X X**

## Game Film: Viewpoint Sets the Stage at Cirque Du Soleil

Walking across the Santa Monica pier, my senses rose to an unusually high level. The misty cool evening air was invigorating after a dinner with great food, new friends and fine wine. As we approached the lit-up big top, I was immediately transported to the thrilling milieu of the circus. Thoughts of lions, tigers, tightrope walkers and clowns immediately flashed through my mind. It was at once familiar and seductive.

After passing the ticket taker and entering the tent, the energy, anticipation and excitement was palpable. And while the concession and souvenir stands were not much different than what you would see at any circus, something in the air was different—this was Cirque Du Soleil. Maybe it was the exotic-looking servers, register clerks and program sellers, or maybe it was the colors and smells…or even magic. Whatever it was, my mind had already begun to move from the circus of my youth to the Cirque Du Soleil experience.

While finding our seats we stared at a giant, translucent egg. Ovo—also the show's title—was center stage. Next a team of exterminators entered the aisles and began slowly pursuing butterflies and other creatures. Exit the exterminators and enter giant crickets while a few fleas and spiders began to climb eight-foot flower stems on the stage. All of this while the tent was still filling with patrons. The stage, still covered by the giant egg, remained a bit of a mystery.

The stage was set and a giant insect egg was hiding a new and exciting world yet to be discovered. I was ready to be amazed.

In its 25th year of thrilling audiences, Cirque du Soleil has mastered the art of creating a worldview, or Viewpoint, that transports audiences to new worlds. By the time the show actually begins, you are a raving fan.

Viewpoint sets the stage and gets us ready to engage our hearts and minds in the experience to come. By building on the familiar and transforming it into a new environment, Cirque Du Soleil does what every marketer dreams of —it creates the perfect playing field from which to deliver against its promise to entertain and amaze.

● ● ● ● ● ● ● ●

# CHAPTER 8

# THE FOUR VIEWPOINT STORY TYPES AND FOUR COMPANIES TELLING THEM WELL

O nce we complete our Viewpoint Story Wheel, we are left with the choice of *how* to tell our story. What do we emphasize and which parts will be most impactful in creating a shared context with our customers that will drive us to Breakthrough when combined with our Value? If we collapse and simplify the story wheel, we can create a 2x2 matrix with four distinct quadrants. Each of these quadrants represents a different lens through which to tell our Viewpoint Story. The four quadrants shown in Figure 17 are labeled *Trendspotting*, *All Pain/No Gain*, *Better Mousetrap* and *Brave New World*. Each is a different lens into the Viewpoint Story Wheel, filtered by two factors: present versus future time and customer versus solution centricity. Each of these story types also map directly to one of the four acts in the Viewpoint Story Wheel.

## THE VIEWPOINT STORY MATRIX

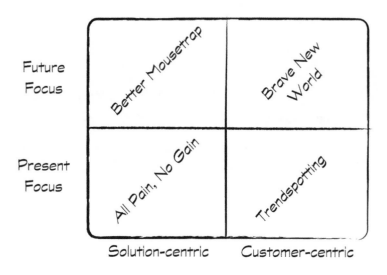

Figure 17: The Viewpoint Story Matrix

All four of these types of Viewpoints can help you stand out and get noticed, creating excellent context for your go-to-market and content-marketing activities. Next we will take a more detailed look at each of these story types, each with an example of a successful company using it, and take a look at their Viewpoint Story Wheel.

## TRENDSPOTTING Story Template

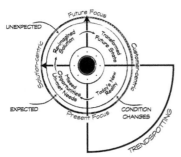

### Filters - Present Focus/Customer-centric

This articulation of a Viewpoint is powerful in that it names and frames an environmental shift that is either keeping the customer up at night or creating great opportunities for them.

### EXAMPLE: Zuora - The Subscription Economy

Zuora coined "The Subscription Economy" effectively owning the name of the megatrend that was engulfing the business world, and have built a highly effective go to market strategy around this articulation. By building the business around The Subscription Economy, Zuora has created a fertile ground for discussing their billing solutions in a context that matters. Rather than simply an accounting solution for selling term licenses, Zuora has effectively planted a flag of leadership. As shown below, Zuora fully fills out their Viewpoint story wheel, but puts a major focus on the trendspotting quadrant. They've even committed a whole website to the discussion of The Subscription Economy. Trendspotting allows Zuora to lead this parade as the expert. Later we

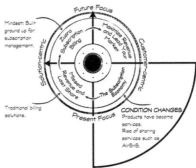

will see how Zuora is leveraging this Viewpoint even further to start a market movement.

**ALL PAIN NO GAIN Story Template**

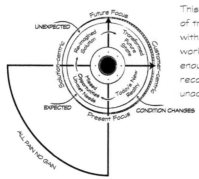

**Filters - Present Focus/Solution-centric**

This articulation focuses on the pain of trying to solve today's big problems with yesterday's solutions. This works great when the pain is large enough to induce action, and is well recognized and acknowledged, yet unaddressed.

**EXAMPLE : FireEye - Modern Malware Exposed**

When FireEye talked about "Modern Malware Exposed" and the resultant risk they created a compelling context for a discussion of their solution. FireEye tapped into a large pain point of organizations, ineffective defense against Modern Malware, and used this Viewpoint story to establish and grow market leadership.

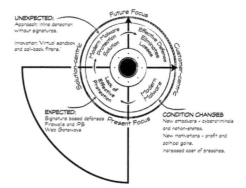

ALL PAIN NO GAIN: FireEye:
Modern Malware Exposed

## A BETTER MOUSETRAP Story Template

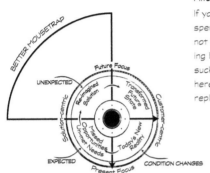

### Filters - Future Focus/Solution-centric

If you know you have a problem, and are spending money to fix it, but either have not eliminated the problem, this positioning leads with, "Hey, what you have sucks and I've got a better solution here." This Viewpoint works great in replacement markets.

## EXAMPLE: Palo Alto Networks - Time to Fix The Firewall

Palo Alto Networks took their "Next Generation Firewall" Viewpoint to the bank to the tune of a $3+B IPO right around the backs of Checkpoint, Fortinet and others. And while arguably those others have caught up with feature sets, Palo Alto is still viewed as the gold standard of the next generation of firewalls. This Better Mousetrap Viewpoint emphasizes the fact that the current solutions are broken and we have a better one. This Viewpoint story type works well for Palo Alto Networks as this market is a primarily a replacement market. In addition, since the founders of Palo Alto were also involved in inventing the "old mousetraps", they speak with great market credibility.

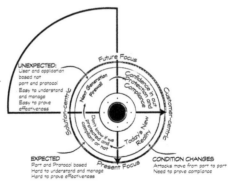

A BETTER MOUSETRAP Palo Alto Networks, It's Time to Fix the Firewall

## BRAVE NEW WORLD Story Template

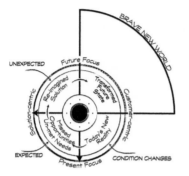

### Filters - Future Focused/Customer-centric

This type of Viewpoint describes the promised new state that the customer can arrive at if they implement your solution. It is powerful because it talks about the intersection of the customer's world and the provider's unique solution.

### Example: Virgin America - Making Flying Fun Again

Flying should be painful, crowded, stressful and miserable. Right? Wrong, says Virgin America. Experience the difference with us. A great example of a Viewpoint which takes conventional wisdom and throws it out the window. This is backed by delivery of the promise of a new and differentiated service. Everything in Virgin's communication is centered around the "fun" of flying with them. To any jaded business or leisure traveler, this is truly a promise of a Brave New World!

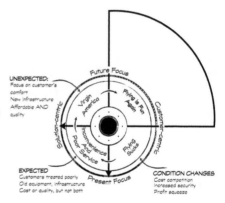

BRAVE NEW WORLD:

Virgin America, Make Flying Fun Again

We have now examined the four Viewpoint Story types. We have seen that with each one fully filling out the Viewpoint Story Wheel, they emphasize a different quadrant. And we have seen examples of successful Viewpoints in each of these four story types. In the next chapter, we will look at a framework for choosing between the four story types to find the right lead for you in your market today.

## The Coach's Corner: The Hero's Journey

In 1949 Joseph Campbell published his groundbreaking and highly influential book, *The Hero with a Thousand Faces*, where he outlined his now famous "Hero's Journey." Campbell proposed that all of our classic tales, from the Odyssey to the biblical Exodus, the stories of the Buddha, Jesus, Prometheus and more followed a similar storyline Campbell calls the "monomyth." According to Campbell, The Hero's Journey, or "monomyth" has 12 stages, which he summarized here:

*A hero ventures forth from the world of common day into a region of supernatural wonder: fabulous forces are there encountered and a decisive victory is won: the hero comes back from this mysterious adventure with the power to bestow boons on his fellow man.*

Campbell's work has influenced scores of modern storytellers such as George Lucas, Stanley Kubrick and J.K. Rowling, and stories as varied as Disney's *Aladdin* to *Watership Down* to the television series *Lost*.

I first came across Campbell's work about five years ago when my daughter's 6th grade social studies curriculum used it as an organizing principal for the year's study. The Viewpoint Story Wheel owes much to Campbell's storytelling model. When I was writing the book, I struggled to build this chapter; I had the ideas and case studies but could not structure them in a way that was repeatable and made sense. Thankfully, my editor Michelle continued to push me to get the model right. In one conversation I told her that this was about the *story*, and all of these "stories" followed the four-act structure you've seen here.

That night, I thought about the Hero's Journey and realized that it was a great way to think about the Viewpoint Story. Here's why:

**Act 1**: Our hero, the customer, is living in a new reality. They may not fully realize it but their world has changed. The first part of our story wheel matches the first part of the monomyth; the hero is jolted from their state of normality into a new reality.

**Act 2**: In the second part, the hero faces seemingly insurmountable challenges in this new world, sinking into depths of despair. This is directly analogous to the All Pain, No Gain section of our Viewpoint Story Wheel.

**Act 3**: Next in the monomyth the hero is granted a magical power, just as our solution grants our customer power in the third part of the Viewpoint Story Wheel.

**Act 4**: Lastly, our hero returns home and transforms it with the magical power they have been granted. Need I say more? Welcome to the Brave New World.

From there it was a small step to create the story wheel framework used in this book. It's not only a great idea to make our customer (not our product) the hero, but it's our responsibility. When we tell the Viewpoint Story, we have the chance to do just that.

We are all on our own personal hero's journey, and my humble and sincere hope is that the Viewpoint Story Wheel can be that magical power that transforms you into a masterful marketing storyteller and helps you to change your company's reality from status quo to market leader.

# CHAPTER 9

# WHICH VIEWPOINT STORIES ARE RIGHT FOR YOU?

**N**ow that you have completed your Viewpoint Story Wheel, we must choose a focus—or story type—for our lead Viewpoint Story execution. As we have seen, all four story types use the full wheel but put emphasis in one of the four areas. So how do we choose what to emphasize?

Well, this depends on a few factors. Often the answer becomes obvious based on the depth and power we see in the story wheel itself. In other cases, we can look at market type and growth dimensions for some guidance.

First, in pure replacement markets we favor the *Better Mousetrap* and *All Pain, No Gain* story types because they are solution-centric, not customer-centric. Conversely, in emerging and new market segments, the *Trendspotting* and *Brave New World* story types are favored because we need to strongly relate to the customer's perspective to get them to act differently.

A second dimension to consider is whether we are in a low- or high-growth market, both from a macro- and micro-economic perspective. In high-growth markets, *Better Mousetrap* and *Brave New World* story types are favored because customers are more likely to already be active in buying cycles. Conversely, in slow-growth markets we favor *Trendspotting* and *All Pain, No Gain*, as these will be more effective in creating new buying cycles. These two dimensions are summarized in Figure 18 below.

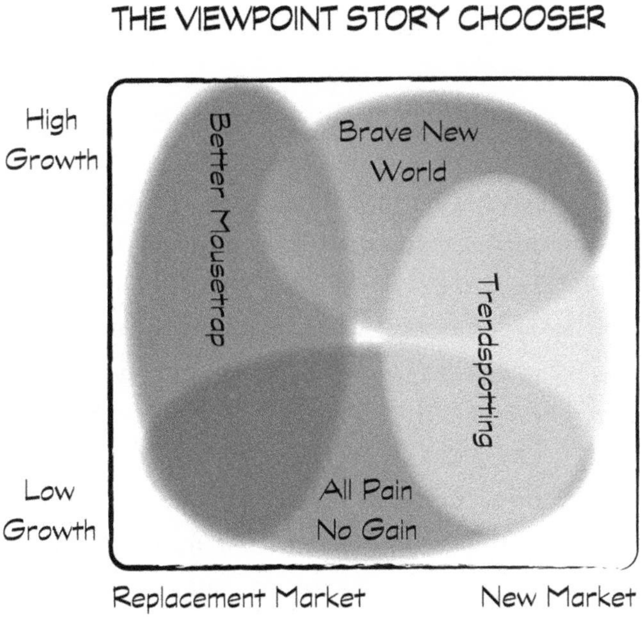

## THE VIEWPOINT STORY CHOOSER

Figure 18: The Viewpoint Story Chooser

Another consideration is market maturity. Because *Trendspotting* and *Brave New World* are more customer-centric than solution-centric, they perform better in early market scenarios where we have a shared interest with our competitors to grow the market. In more mature markets, *All Pain, No Gain* and *Better Mousetrap* can often be effective where market share capture is more critical than total market growth.

In general, when building Viewpoint stories that are customer-centric, we must make sure we include enough of the left side quadrants in our narrative to ground it in our solution space rather than letting it drift to a generic market or vision discussion. Conversely, when building solution-centric Viewpoints, we *must* include enough of the trends and future state to keep this a context rather than pure product story. As with most skills, Viewpoint storytelling takes work and practice. The examples and frameworks in the last three chapters are meant to shortcut your work and get you to a powerful, draft Viewpoint to test, refine and deploy in your market.

If we want another filter on this choice, it's helpful to think in terms of the Hero's Journey metaphor we discussed at the end the last chapter.

**Act 1 *Trendspotting* stories** jolt our hero out of a state of complacency and alert them to the fact that the world around them has changed. We gain credibility by pointing out what might seem obvious but is not labeled or spoken of. Zuora, as we saw in the example, labeled what now seems an obvious trend: The Subscription Economy. This really helped buyers understand their new reality that they felt but had not named.

**Act 2 *All Pain, No Gain*** stories take our hero into the depths of despair because they are in pain or missing important opportunities. While we see that this can work well in markets like IT security, we must be careful that this does not come across as fear mongering or scare tactics. This type of story is effective when it is communicated more in the language of risk and missed opportunity than fear and loss.

**Act 3 *Better Mousetrap*** stories imbue our hero with the magical power of our new solution. The more new and radically innovative our solution is, the more powerful this approach can be. Magic must communicate wonder and while our AIM framework can be effective in articulating "magic," wonder is hard to create with messaging. When the product user or buyer has an *oh, wow!* reaction, then this type of story can be highly effective, as was the case with Palo Alto Networks.

**Act 4 *Brave New World*** stories are the most transformative and inspiring, as they help our hero transform their company and industry. In high-growth, new markets or when the transformation is large, this can be a very effective lead-story type. Our Hero's Journey has brought us home.

By creating a unique Viewpoint, we create the space or the context to deliver our unique Value. So with that contextual foundation laid, let's now shift from building a Viewpoint Story to defining unique Value. We will then combine these two things to reach the Breakthrough stage of our Market Leadership journey.

## CHAPTER 10
# TILTING TO ABUNDANCE

I n his seminal work *The Seven Habits of Highly Successful People*, Steven Covey introduces a concept he calls the Abundance Mentality. Covey's idea means that we believe there is enough success to share with others. He contrasts it with the Scarcity Mentality, where we believe that if someone else wins, it means we lose—not considering the possibility of everyone being capable of winning (in some way or another) in a given situation.

When we apply this idea to go-to-market positioning, messaging and execution, we begin to see our opportunities in a whole new way and drive an execution that can surprise even our most optimistic expectations.

Value is the articulation of our winning business benefits that we use to move potential customers from awareness to purchase ready. Once we get their attention with our Viewpoint, we need to rapidly captivate them with our Unique Value conversation.

Value: The Business benefits that a solution delivers for which customers are willing to pay both real and opportunity costs to acquire.

Unique Value: A value that only comes from us, not other alternatives in the market.

So, what are the three steps to articulating Unique Value and using it to sneak up on and beat our competitors without them even knowing it?

Step 1) Adopt an abundance mentality. The abundance mentality simply says that we view our market not as a competitive dogfight for a finite and scarce amount of business, but as a unlimited landscape of opportunity. When we do this, we change our perspective from battle to maneuver and our focus from better to different.

Step 2) Invest the time and energy to do the mechanics of building out Value and its articulation in powerful messaging and positioning. We do this by starting with an honest assessment of our uniqueness. After completing the process in the previous chapter, we use that output to create well documented and customer-validated positioning and messaging. There are many formats for messaging and positioning documentation and you may have one you already prefer. A version of these that I use is available for download on kenrutsky.com.

Step 3) We then tilt the playing field to our advantage by changing the terrain from conventional wisdom to our Viewpoint. When our Viewpoint creates the context for the customer and market conversations, the diagram changes to look more like this:

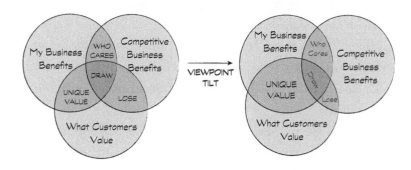

Figure 19: Viewpoint Tilts the Playing Field

## Game Film: Palo Alto Networks Tilts the Playing Field

Palo Alto Networks provides an excellent example of Unique Value in action. Security folks have long recognized that firewalls were providing less and less protection as more and more network traffic went over the Web protocol. Nearly all firewalls have traditionally allowed Web traffic through, as if the door to your office let anyone dressed in a business suit in without regards to their intent. But it took courage when Palo Alto Networks stepped out and claimed that "the firewall is broken" (Viewpoint), but they could fix it with three key protection features. Did this anger customers who were writing millions of dollars in checks to Check Point, McAfee, Juniper and Cisco? Some yes, but others apparently not, as it soon becomes clear.

At the time of their initial launch, I was running network security marketing for Secure Computing, now part of McAfee. I can remember the product manager telling me that "Palo Alto is nothing but a web-filtering box; it's not a real firewall." So while McAfee, Check Point and others fought over the percentage points of share in the old firewall market, Palo Alto Networks titled the playing field by articulating their

Viewpoint and Unique Value and executing it with excellence. Sure, the others eventually noticed, but it may have simply been too late. Now, seven years later, Palo Alto Networks has disrupted a stagnant market, grown from zero to more than $1B in revenue, executed a highly successful IPO in 2012 and is valued at over $13B on the public markets. In fact, in the five years since the IPO, Palo Alto Networks' stock price has nearly tripled and their market cap is now equal to the then dominant incumbent, Check Point, all from fixing the firewall!

As an aside, to tell if the market is being tilted on you, your best sales reps are usually the canary in the coalmine. I vividly remember a sales manager in my office saying, "We need an answer to Palo Alto." I replied with, "Really? What are they, $10M out of $3B right now? Let's keep an eye on the real competition." Boy did I get that one wrong!

● ● ● ● ● ● ● ● ●

# The Coach's Corner:
# Scaling Your Viewpoint Story

Let's now use the scaling framework from Chapter 5 to look at how we can scale our Viewpoint Story. Let's say we have built an Act 1, Trendspotting Viewpoint Story. How would we scale and utilize that story in our go-to-market execution?

### Step 1: Build Out Our Content
First we take our Viewpoint Story and scale it down and up. Here are a couple high-impact examples.

- **Scale Down**: We build a library of tweets that talk about the new reality. For each condition change we identified in our

STEEP process, we build five tweets. This gives us 15-20 tweets about the new reality.

- **Scale Up**: Taking our four-act story, we write and publish and e-book. We then create derivative content repurposing our story. For example, we create an infographic that supports each of our four acts.

### Step 2: Find Our Voices

We fill out our library with blogs, case studies, and other stories and data that support our Viewpoint Story. Our experts create interesting spins on our Viewpoint. We engage outside experts to provide their perspectives. By taking our core message and changing its size and voice, we now have dozens of possible executions of our core Viewpoint Story. One of the most effective ways to drive awareness, retention and preference is repetition. By scaling our core message down, up and out, we gain a full quiver of arrows to send into the market.

### Step 3: Build Our Channels

We now have dozens of content assets in various sizes, voices and formats. Now we can put our demand generation, content marketing and programs teams to work. We are confident we have a story that matters; now we just need to get it out there and use it.

### Step 4: Wash, Rinse, Repeat

Why stop there? Our Viewpoint Story Wheel has four acts. We can now pick a second act to build content around. In our example, we started with the new reality. We can now move to either of the adjacent acts and begin telling that story. What's the Brave New World we can take the customer to? Write that e-book. What are the unmet needs of the market? Blog about that and commission a third-party study that backs your hypothesis with hard data. Then continue this process until you have a rich library of assets across all four acts of your Viewpoint Story.

The purpose of this Coach's Corner is not to teach you content marketing or demand generation; however, we have invested a lot to build the Viewpoint Story that matters. This demonstrates for you the rich palette of options you have to tell that story. The same steps are then applied to your Unique Value messages from Chapter 4. As you see, there is no excuse for not having enough to say that matters. If you build a Viewpoint Story Wheel and a set of Unique Value propositions, scaling is a matter of activity and effort—something great marketing teams have always had to excel at.

# THE SECOND HALF PLAYBOOK— LEADERSHIP

## CHAPTER 11

# SHOW ME, DON'T TELL ME!

Today, nearly all high-quality, go-to-market programs tailor their delivery to channels of communication and to where the customer is in the buying cycle. *Content Rules,* by Handley and Chapman—a popular book in marketing circles—spends a lot of time focusing on just that; and it is necessary and recommended reading and table stakes for today's marketer. Effective content marketing also uses the scaling concepts covered here in Chapter 5 and in the Coach's Corner at the end of the previous chapter.

However, stopping there would fail to take on the other two variables in the equation:

Engagement and Experience. If you have content without context, buyers won't listen or care. Even after telling the most important story—your Viewpoint Story—using it to drive home your Unique Value and reach the Participation stage, you must continue on the Market Leadership journey to the Breakthrough stage. Building on our Value, Viewpoint and scaled-up and scaled-down messaging, we must then increase the level of Engagement and Experience we deliver in our marketing programs and communications.

We can look at both Engagement and Experience as continuums. Engagement measures the level of interaction that the customer has with our content; we are most engaged when we are interacting, least when we are reading. Engagement, through multiple senses and interaction, creates memorable content-marketing engagements.

From an Experience perspective, we can describe or demonstrate our Value, or have the customer participate in understanding the Value. Communication of Value via Experience is vastly more effective at winning customers' preference than description.

Velocity, as shown in Figure 20, is the combination of high-engagement, high-participation programs. Clearly, we should strive for a mix of high- and low-velocity deliverables. There are times, especially in highly technical markets, where the whitepaper is a key component of the marketing deliverables mix. But even then, most whitepapers are so bad they put the audience to sleep. But here, we focus on the upper-right reaches of the Velocity Execution Model.

For example, well executed and managed trial programs, where we engage directly in the customer's buying journey, are far more effective in converting prospects than a whitepaper describing the benefits of that journey.

Conventional wisdom in B2B sales tends to argue against standard demonstrations of value early in the sales or buying cycle. The first objection is rooted in the solution/diagnostic-selling mindset that says until we can specifically describe the Value of our solution and customize the demo, we should not show the product. Contrast this approach to Breakthrough Marketing, where the

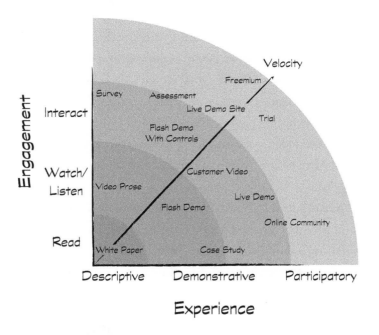

Figure 20: Engagement and Experience Create Velocity

company has established a context for discussing the Value of their product, then proudly points the customer to an online demo in that context.

In the meantime, our solution-selling counterpart is still establishing need with the customer, who will now view everything in the context of the first provider. That's a tough sell. The Viewpoint adherent has established and tilted the playing field in their direction.

The second objection to showing interactive demos is commonly that "our product is just too hard to demo without someone from our team showing it." Let's take a quick look at several case studies that strongly refute both of these claims.

# Game Film: Nimsoft Accelerates Sales Cycles with Online Demo

Nimsoft, a provider of IT monitoring products and SaaS services was facing a critical juncture in 2009. Positioned as a "me too" provider, Nimsoft's tagline was "The Big 4 Alternative," alluding to the fact that they were easier and less costly to implement than the four traditional large providers in that market space.

They created a high-impact go-to-market positioning around "Unified Monitoring, from the Data Center to the Cloud." This was backed by a well thought out and articulated set of go-to-market messages around this Viewpoint that drove their Value home. Most importantly, they created an online marketing demonstration hub at www.unifiedmonitoring.com, which allowed customers and prospects to see unified monitoring in action. A screenshot is shown in Figure 21.

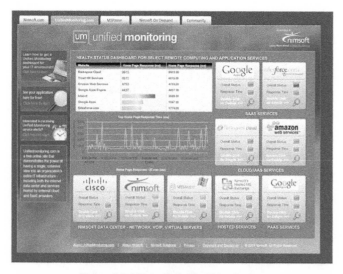

Figure 21: Nimsoft Unified Monitoring

Traditionally in their market, demos were customized and delivered in the third, fourth or fifth sales engagement, and then when a systems engineer could be scheduled. This process normally took as long as 4–6 weeks from lead to demo. Once the Unified Monitoring demo portal was launched, sales reps would demo this as part of the first call. This did three things for Nimsoft. First, it cut up to four weeks out of the sales cycle. Second, it showed the prospect the business value of the Unified Monitoring approach in a dramatic way. And lastly, it tilted the playing field strongly in Nimsoft's direction, putting them in the pole position for the sale. Nimsoft's parade was lead by this high-velocity implementation of their Viewpoint Story.

This high-impact, high-velocity approach positioned Nimsoft for both growth and the eventual acquisition by CA, Inc. in March of 2010.

● ● ● ● ● ● ● ● ●

## Game Film: Dog Food and Stone Skipping—Something Quirky

Figure 22: Eat the Dog Food

Jim Barksdale was the CEO of Netscape when I worked there in the late 1990s. One of the things that makes Jim an amazing leader is his homespun, southern storytelling and sayings, which made him the most quotable CEO I've ever known. Work for him for a few years and you leave with a small library of "Barksdalisms." One of Jim's sayings was, "It ain't dog food unless the dog comes off the porch to eat it."

While Jim's point was that you can love your product but if the customer doesn't buy it, it isn't worth much, I don't think Jim ever intended to be taken literally. German pet-food manufacturer GranataPet did just that. Grenata implemented a mobile-enabled, dog-food-dispensing billboard where they delivered the experience and value of their food directly to their end customer. When the customer checked in with their mobile device, the billboard would automatically dispense a sample of dog food–hopefully the dog would like it!

Have you ever felt like escaping the doldrums of your computer, sitting down by a mountain lake and skipping stones? That's exactly the experience that San Francisco design firm Eleven Inc. created in their SkipTown promo for Sun Valley, Idaho. They set up a website featuring Skippy, the world's first (and maybe only?) web-controlled,

Figure 23: Skip a Stone

stone-skipping robot. Would be vacationers could experience Sun Valley in the summer—the key objective of the campaign.

When I hear that software, SaaS and other B2B companies hide their product or services experience behind rationalizations and excuses such as the belief that the customer will not see enough "value" in the trial or demo experience, or that competitors will learn too much and thereby gain an advantage, I want to fire up these two videos from the Coach's Corner. That's showing value. That's having the customer be part of the experience. If Sun Valley and Granata can do it, so can you!

So whether you are selling dog food, mountain vacations or a B2B product, there's a way to accelerate your pipeline today by adding experience and engagement to your marketing mix. Don't get stuck in the typical bottom left of B2B marketing programs and deliverables. Breaking through requires breaking out of that old mindset, pattern and approach.

● ● ● ● ● ● ● ● ●

## CHAPTER 12

# BREAKTHROUGH SALES— WINNING AT THE COALFACE

**B**2B marketers have a reputation for sitting in the office and dreaming stuff up. Whether or not this is deserved, they're seen as being disconnected from the coalface frontline of dealing with customers while they drift in a theoretical world of slogans and campaign plans. On the other hand, B2B sales reps have a reputation for being tactical and short-term focused. In many ways they have to be focused on closing the current deal before they can move on. However, the truth is that the best of both sales and marketing folks are converging in a common framework, one that has long-term perspective or context *and* short-term value and experience, delivered with Velocity.

Breakthrough sales is the natural extension of our Breakthrough Marketing framework. Breakthrough-driven sales reps are strategically driven by Viewpoint and tactically driven by demonstrating and delivering Value to customers. Today's high performing B2B sales reps keep these three principles in mind.

1.  Establish a shared context with the customer
2.  Teach the customer and enable them to be a teacher, too
3.  Never hesitate to demonstrate the Value of the product, service or solution

This represents, in many ways, a radical departure from traditional "solution/diagnostic selling" to more expert- and authority-driven selling. In the old school, an initial conversation might look like this:

Joe (solution-selling rep): *"Hi Carl, I'd like to understand what you are doing about problem X in your business?"*

Carl (customer): *"Well Joe, what does your product do and how can it help me?"*

Joe: *"Sure, we have an X, but before I tell you how it can help, can we spend 30 minutes where I can ask you some questions?"*

Reps who try this technique today are often shown the door before they even get started. First of all, customers expect the rep to know their business *before* arrival and second, they already know about the product from their network or research online prior to the sales call. Successful reps transition that first conversation to this:

Jane (Breakthrough sales rep): *"Hi Carl, I'd love to talk to you a bit about our perspective on issues/opportunities X, Y and Z facing our industry, and how our solution is helping organizations just like yours in this new world. Do you have five minutes?"*

Carl: *"Sure, but please make it quick, I have a lot on my plate."*

Jane: *"No problem. What we see is that customers like you now live in a world like…" (tells her Viewpoint Story, teaching the customer and creating a shared context)."*

Whether you call this Solution Selling 2.0, The Challenger Sale or something else, the fact of the matter is, buyers already know about your product's features and functions from your website. They need the *why*. Great sales reps establish and reinforce the why from the very beginning of the sales cycle.

The value of this to the sales rep is immense. First, they gain a foothold in establishing the context of the sales conversation. When they transition to describing and demonstrating value, they do so in this shared context.

Second, they have established their personal credibility and value with the customer by teaching the customer something meaningful.

Third, they have begun to lay the groundwork for establishing why their solution is not only valuable, but strategic. Before a buyer can make the decision to purchase, they have to consider *and* prioritize your solution. Traditional solution selling doesn't help much here. Only by creating context can sales reps rise above the noise to the top of the priority list.

Lastly, they have armed Carl with the knowledge he needs to spread the context within his organization. Every conversation starts with context, whether from Carl or Jane. Jane transfers her expertise to Carl, who then uses it to establish and drive the sale internally within the organization. Carl becomes the context champion to help Jane influence and accelerate the buying process.

Later, in our traditional solution-selling process, we'd likely have this conversation:

Carl: *"Can I see a demo of your solution?"*

Joe: *"Sure, Carl. But before we do that, I'd really like to understand your goals a bit better. And I'd like to know when you think you can make a purchase decision. And I want to make sure the budget is in place. And I'd like to understand the entire procurement process. Then after I know all that, I can schedule my solution engineer/manager/consultant to show you the demo."*

And while Joe waits and qualifies until he is satisfied, Carl has already implemented the online trial version of Jane's competitive solution. Carl is busy experiencing the Value and Jane is establishing control of the sale at Joe's expense.

Breakthrough sales reps are thrilled and enthusiastic about revealing information early in the process when the opportunity may not be fully qualified, because they understand if they can control the context and manage the perception of value effectively in that context. And if they have confidence in the value of their solution, then having Carl experience the value can do *nothing* bad and a lot of good. It will accelerate and grow the deal far faster than Joe's qualification solution strategy does.

Clearly, the Breakthrough rep needs marketing's help. She must be armed with the Viewpoint Story with the ability to articulate the Value of the solution in that context. She must also have the tools to demonstrate that Value throughout the buying cycle. The journey to market leadership is a shared journey between sales and marketing teams.

## CHAPTER 13

# BREAKTHROUGH MARKETING AND THE MODERN MARKETER

This book has been written for the modern B2B marketer. We have seen how successful companies use a Viewpoint-, Value- and Experience-driven approach to stand out in today's crowded and information-overloaded market. We have seen how companies creating context for the Value discussion can tilt the playing field to their advantage. And we have seen how experience-driven marketing, when coupled with Unique Value and message scaling, can create and accelerate buying cycles.

Yet it would seem that we have not discussed what seem to be the hottest topics in today's marketing community: content marketing, market automation and so-called "growth hacking." However, as you will see, Breakthrough Marketing is not only good for the successful modern marketer, it is *essential*. Whether viewed as the key ingredient of the content-marketing recipe, the fuel of great marketing automation or the guidelines and payoff of a growth hacking initiative, the frameworks and principles covered here enable modern marketers to not only survive and compete, but to thrive and lead in their markets. With a strong Viewpoint, defined Unique Value and Experience-driven delivery, content marketing brings relevant and meaningful insight to customers; marketing automation thrives with the fuel it needs; and growth-hacking initiatives are correctly targeted and executed. Let's take a quick look at each of these.

## Content Marketing

> *"Content Marketing is a strategic marketing approach focused on creating and distributing valuable, relevant, and consistent content to attract and retain a clearly-defined audience—and, ultimately, to drive profitable customer action"*
> — Content Marketing Institute

As we saw earlier in the CMI study, the number-one challenge identified by content marketing teams was producing enough engaging and relevant content! Fortunately, the Breakthrough Marketing practitioner is well equipped to drive engaging content because he has targeted his most important story—the Viewpoint Story—directly into the strike zone of the targeted buyer's relevance zone. In fact, a well-articulated Viewpoint can serve as a wealth of relevant content. As we have seen, we can take each point on the Viewpoint Story Wheel and scale content up and out.

First, take your Viewpoint Story and scale it up as an e-book and infographic. Then dissect each piece of the e-book and scale it up and out. In doing so, make sure that you apply the principles from the Experience framework to build both engagement and interaction into your content deliverables. Then apply the same process to each of your key value statements.

Viewpoint and Value are the key ingredients for creating relevant and valuable content. Applying the principles of this book can enable the content marketer to successfully navigate the biggest challenge to content marketing success: producing engaging content.

## Marketing Automation

*"Marketing Automation refers to the software platforms and technologies designed for marketing departments and organizations to more effectively market on multiple channels online (such as email, social media, websites, etc.) and automate repetitive tasks."*
—Wikipedia

*"Marketing automation is a category of technology that allows companies to streamline, automate, and measure marketing tasks and workflows, so they can increase operational efficiency and grow revenue faster."*
— Marketo

No part of marketing has changed more in the last decade than the technology and automation of marketing campaigns and processes. From email list managers and campaign managers, we have evolved to lead-scoring, lead-management, advanced-targeting and account-based marketing, and deep integration with salesforce automation and processes. With this change, we've become more and more science and metric driven.

We have built an incredible machine—a Ferrari of marketing efficiency and capability. Content and data are the fuels that power the marketing-automation machine. With low-quality fuel (i.e.

data or content), the machine is prone to knocks, misfires and poor performance. Great content, as we just saw, must be valuable and relevant. Breakthrough Marketing provides high-test fuel for your marketing automation machine.

## Growth Hacking

> *"Growth hacking is a marketing technique developed by technology startups which use creativity, analytical thinking, and social metrics to sell products and gain exposure. It can be seen as part of the online marketing ecosystem, as in many cases growth hackers are using techniques such as search engine optimization, website analytics, content marketing and A/B testing. Growth hackers focus on low-cost and innovative alternatives to traditional marketing, e.g. utilizing social media and viral marketing instead of buying advertising."*
>
> — Wikipedia

Perhaps no term has generated more buzz and excitement in the technology-marketing world than "growth hacking." In fact, in his seminal blog entitled, "Growth Hacker is the New VP Marketing," Andrew Chen went as far as to declare the VP of marketing dead.

There is no doubt that in B2C online businesses, growth hacking (i.e. integration of your service into others), often via APIs, is a creative and powerful way to do customer acquisition. However, in the B2B world where sales are multi-tier and complex, growth hacking has had a far more mixed reception. Some would argue that this is due to entrenched marketing teams and models, "old" approaches and little flexibility.

The truth, as it normally does, lies somewhere in the middle. Marketing, especially direct marketing, has always been part science, and business development has always been about partnering and distribution. There has been a continued rise of analytics in marketing starting with direct marketing, moving to SEO/SEM and continuing with the emerging fields of social analytics, A/B testing and other new techniques. As mentioned, to many CEOs marketing is no longer a "black art" but a "black science."

In today's overloaded information market, getting attention is still about context and communications. The argument that coders and data scientists will be the only types of marketers in the future is just a leap beyond logic and reality. Marketing, taken in its broader sense, is the understanding of markets, buyers, communication and value exchange. Breakthrough Marketing provides a powerful way to articulate this understanding in the marketplace. Our Viewpoint can form not only the basis for our external communications, but a way to explain our Value to our internal teams, including the "growth hackers" tasked with effectively integrating us into alternative channels and platforms to drive customer education and acquisition.

The Final Drive

# WINNING THE CHAMPION'S CUP— TRANSFORMATION

## CHAPTER 14

# BEYOND BREAKTHROUGH—FLASHMOBS, PARADES AND MOVEMENTS

**M**arket leadership is a desirable goal. So far we have discussed Breakthrough and leadership as our goals in driving more results from our B2B marketing efforts. We've talked about creating a powerful Viewpoint, defining our Unique Value and combining these two to tilt the market to our advantage. We've also discussed scaling our messaging and adding a large experiential component to our communications in order to create leadership. In order to complete the picture, we now need to introduce the concept of a market-leadership lifecycle.

There is no question about it; market leaders are more valuable than followers and that's always been the case. However, in today's crowded markets, there are leaders and losers, but not much in between. Unfortunately, new entrants are really faced with an uphill battle in establishing market leadership. First of all, there is often an established category and leader. Unseating leaders is challenging because we find ourselves fighting on their terrain instead of our own. B2B buyers are a conservative bunch, and their bias is often to buy from the established leader. As they say, no one ever got fired over buying from IBM. This is even true in newer markets where leaders like Google or Salesforce.com may be a more attractive supplier to conservative buyers than a newly funded or smaller competitor. Lastly, becoming known as a start-up has historically been a long and very expensive proposition, requiring heavy resources in brand building, PR and people.

However, the change in information availability and independent buyers has created a new and exciting dynamic for both smaller and newer B2B-market entrants. They can use new techniques of inbound and content marketing to create presence and preference. The barriers to content creation and distribution have fallen dramatically, creating the *possibility* of breaking through. Start-ups no longer need to accept playing second fiddle, but the smart and savvy ones can create market leadership via flashmobs, parades and movements.

The path of market leadership looks like Figure 24, with three phases that the typical leader goes through in their path to success.

Each of these three phases has different characteristics and approaches. Fortunately, this journey coincides with the Market Leadership Achievement Ladder we described in Chapter 1. In fact, we can overlay these market leadership phases directly over our Market Leadership Journey as shown in Figure 25. And as you see, we've added a final stage to our journey—Transformation—which we will discuss briefly here.

### Stage 6: Transformation
When we climb the last step of the ladder, we are now a leader who is actively transforming the marketplace. We have earned rabid fans

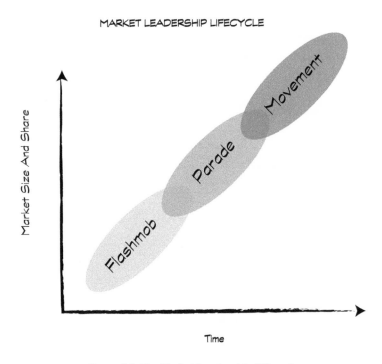

Figure 24: The Market Leadership Lifecycle

by articulating compelling Value and Viewpoint, aligned in such a way that they're compelled to learn more and impact the market. We have then mastered the art of executing with experiential and high-impact programs and are now the recognized market leader in our segment. We can then begin to drive our transformational purpose into our messaging and positioning, enabling us to not only build our original market segment, but to quickly expand into related and adjacent segments, markets and solutions. As we elevate our story, we elevate our opportunity. Leads flow in and conversions skyrocket. Transformational leaders enjoy a huge advantage over their product-centric messaging competitors.

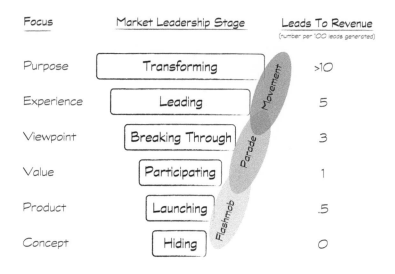

Figure 25: The Extended Market Leadership Journey

Let's now use the lens of market leadership phases to further understand how to use the concepts of Breakthrough Marketing to accelerate this journey.

## Flashmobs: The beginning path to market leadership

Flashmobs are the first phase of the market-leadership lifecycle. Flashmobs, as the name implies, are relatively small groups of passionate customers who share a common interest, problem or need. Our goal during this phase is to find and capture this committed group of customers. These are the customers who are highly attuned to our value and willing to go against the flow of mainstream adopters. The key to capturing a Flashmob is a well-defined and targeted set of Unique Value statements presented in a well-targeted context or Viewpoint. These early customers then act as sales reps for your team, building a Flashmob of demand and creating new leaders out of the acceleration of end-user and subsequent enterprise adoption. They switch jobs and refer to peers in other organizations—network effects that grow both presence and users—and they build your early market leadership.

Flashmobs can be a significant driver of moving from hiding to breaking through; by developing and scaling Viewpoint- and Value-based messaging, we can attract and engage with our early market customers and create one or more flashmobs. For example, we may create a different Flashmob for each of our core Unique Value statements. Or we may create industry specific flashmobs. Let's take a quick look at one example.

### Game Film: DMTI Creates a Flashmob— From Key Customer Acquisition to Being Acquired

In 2012 I helped a client, DMTI Spatial, establish a new Viewpoint called "Location Economics." DMTI was the market leader in Canadian GIS data; however, to build new revenue streams and increase the business value, they needed to increase new customer acquisition by selling value beyond the database. After going through the Viewpoint Story Wheel process, their *Brave New World Act 4* story went something like this:

> "Today we live in a mobile society. The movement of people, things and information creates both opportunity and risk. If you can integrate location information that is timely and accurate into your critical business and customer facing transactions, you can unlock the power of Location Economics, increasing revenues and reducing risk."

This led to a new set of key customers and referrals—the creation of a Flashmob. In 2013, European market leader Neopost successfully acquired DMTI. Below is a brief email Q&A I held with former DMTI President, Phil Kazuba, about the value of DMTI's Viewpoint Story process.

**What were the most valuable outcomes and take-aways from the project?**

Clarity, focus and purpose. The process helped the leadership team establish our unique viewpoint in a market that was highly fragmented with point solutions. Once that was established, it created an opportunity for focus and helped the entire organization, its customers and prospects to appreciate the "purpose" we had as an entity.

**How did the results impact the DMTI business?**

This process spurred us to successfully complete our migration from a data-services company to a SaaS company focused on helping our clients create economic value through the intelligent use of location. I believe the vision was also one of the key reasons DMTI was acquired by Neopost.

**What was the most unique aspect of the project and the value you got from it?**

The process was hard work; there are no shortcuts. But going through it truly helped all aspects of the organization—leadership, product management, marketing, sales and development. Though I wish we had committed earlier to implementing, in the end, we were able to articulate a unique viewpoint to our targeted audience and secure new, key influential customers who in return became advocates of our vision and highly referenceable clients. We truly did take market leadership and it paid off in real and tangible business value for our company, customers and shareholders.

● ● ● ● ● ● ● ● ●

### Parades: "If you want to be a leader, find a parade and get in front of it," Walt Kelly's Pogo

Parades are the phase where you are defining and leading a broader market category. Your initial Flashmob has grown and is moving, attracting new groups of buyers who notice the activity noise and success of the crowd—with your help of course! This phase of market leadership is very context-sensitive. Winners are the ones who articulate a compelling Viewpoint, most often of the *New Reality* or *Brave New World* type.

More so than ever, we're living in a tumultuous and ever-changing world, and B2B buyers are no exception; new challenges and opportunities for both individuals and organizations come at a dizzying pace. At the root of this is a set of changes that create context for just about everything. Examples of some of the technology, meta-context-changing items in B2B markets include: BigData, The Mobile Society and SaaS. Other meta-contexts can be more cultural, like privacy; or economic like the increases in income inequality; or environmental like climate change. Our STEEP analysis from Chapter 7 helps us to understand and define which of these meta-contexts matter the most to our target customers. In order to lead the parade, we "hook on" to one or more of these contexts and build our Viewpoint Story around these. We become leaders of the parades and then customers and market share follow. Parade leaders grow quickly and gain share as category leaders.

From Participation to Breakthrough, it's *parades* that build our market leadership. We have a crowd that is actively choosing to follow us, as opposed to mindlessly following the majority. By shifting our conversation more to Viewpoint and increasing our Experience delivery, we energize and grow our flashmobs into our market parade.

 ## Game Film: GoodData Marshals a Parade—Messaging to Win in a Crowded Market

Business Intelligence (BI) is an established, large and growing market, but it is also a changing and fluid one, impacted by many of the trendy words you might hear like Big Data, Hadoop, IOT, Cloud and many others. It's crowded with established vendors ranging from IBM to SAP, new successes like 2013 IPO Tableau (DATA on NYSE, Mktg. Cap 6B+!) and just acquired by Hitachi Data Systems' Pentaho (for a reported $500-600M). Among the biggest trends in the space is "BI in the Cloud." One of the innovators in moving BI into the cloud is the San Francisco-based company GoodData. Founded in 2007, GoodData has been a darling of Sand Hill Road, having raised a reported total of more than $100M in venture from stellar firms including Andreessen Horowitz and Intel Capital. Life is good when you are the leader of a big trend in a big market.

However, "BI in the Cloud" is a tenuous leadership positioning. Everyone is already in or is moving to the cloud. And while Salesforce.com could leverage its first-to-the-cloud advantage to not only lead but transform an entire market, competitors will not fall easily for that one anymore. Customers, while wanting cloud first, now expect it and want to know why you matter to them more than everyone else does.

So, rather than rest on the strategy of being the "Leader in Cloud BI," or "BI as a Service," GoodData recently transitioned its positioning to being the leading provider of an "Analytics Distribution Platform." To quote their website: "GoodData enables Enterprises and ISVs to transform their businesses by distributing targeted analytics to every stakeholder across their business networks."

In short, GoodData offers you a (much) Better Mousetrap! It's not just about moving the cheese to the cloud, it's about a new way to find and capture business value. This is classic parade-leadership positioning. An analytics distribution platform is a different approach—a different mindset—and is driven by a set of innovative features. GoodData is essentially saying: We are re-inventing BI in the Cloud, calling it an Analytics Distribution Platform, our new mousetrap. And with that, we will deliver you to the Brave New World that "unlocks the value of your data, letting you reap the rewards of one-to-many analytics."

I have described in detail a process that helps companies create a unique and market-leading Viewpoint and I applaud both the courage and the strategy that GoodData is pursuing in declaring a new positioning—essentially, the distribution of analytics to unlock business value. Today, customers are driven to find and take advantage of their data to unlock new business opportunities. Traditional BI is focused on the analyst, not the extended enterprise. By positioning itself as an Analytics Distribution Platform provider, not only does GoodData stand out from competitors, it exactly aligns with the value that customers are trying to get. This is a bold attempt to lead the market forward. If they are successful, my belief is that the $100M venture investment will be a small fraction of the value created.

### Interview with GoodData's CEO, Roman Stanek

Analytics Distribution, as GoodData describes it, is a much better mousetrap than BI in the Cloud. To lead a market, you need to define the context of the conversation, and GoodData is trying to do just that. I discussed this new positioning with Roman Stanek via email; his answers provide more insight into how and why GoodData is pursuing this strategy.

**What led the need to change GoodData's positioning to Analytics Distribution?**

Our goal was to move the discussion away from technologies— especially vendor comparisons—so that we could talk about the real values that we are providing to our customers. Talking to CEOs about unlocking the value of their data to create revenue and new business is sure a lot more meaningful.

**How did you come up with the new positioning?**

We looked at why we, and many of our current customers, were succeeding with GoodData and the common attributes became very obvious. The customers who were getting the most value out of our products were the ones who were extending the analytics to broader audiences, both internally and externally. It became about unlocking business value and even about creating new products and services, not about analysts doing analyses.

**Why should customers care about an Analytics Distribution Platform?**

BI is BI. We do a great job of it and are extremely proud of our ability to deliver insight to customers very quickly, but BI for the sake of analysis pales in comparison to creating and scaling new and existing products based on the data you have. Every business has data that is more valuable if it can be unlocked as insight and distributed to audiences for which it creates value. However, until now, doing this was prohibitively expensive and complex because IT organizations had to custom build every implementation and often failed in the process. We have productized this approach and therefore enabled businesses to do this quickly and cost effectively.

**Why wasn't "BI in the Cloud" or "BI as a Service" a good enough description?**

It really didn't characterize the value we bring. BI just sounds like tools and database drivers and we go far beyond that.

**Where do you see the messaging evolving to over time?**

We see it becoming bigger and more encompassing. We think other vendors will copy it and help us build out this space in the market. But the collective intelligence we have amassed and are continually growing is uniquely ours.

**What's the magical place you can take customers to who come with you on this journey?**

Their magical place is being the leader in their market, where they have unlocked amazing value from the operational business data they already have.

● ● ● ● ● ● ● ● ●

## Movements: Some contexts are SO big that they become movements

Movements are bigger than parades. They don't simply last a day, week or year, but can last for a decade. Movements are the things we remember when we look back on our history, like "The Internet" or "Mobile Computing." Movements have many leaders; the Civil Rights Movement had leaders as varying as Martin Luther King, Jr., Rosa Parks and Malcolm X. Large-market movements are made up of many related parades and the leaders of each of these parades usually vie with each other to consolidate their movements under their leadership. Salesforce.com has parlayed its SaaS/CRM parade leadership to emerge as the leader of the entire sales and marketing automation movement. FireEye is in the process of trying to leverage its parade leadership in "Advanced Network Threat Protection" into a new movement to "Re-Imagine Security" around their brand and technology.

Within these movements we see the constant bubbling up of new flashmobs, parades and the spawning of other movements. Leaders find ways to create flashmobs, get in front of parades and then use their successes to build movements. Small vendors can emerge in ways that seem inconceivable outside this process, but those who understand it can take use it to thrive in today's hyper-competitive markets, becoming product, category and market leaders.

Movements are driven by purpose, and that's what takes us from leadership to transformation. When your purpose aligns clearly with that of your customer, they can't do anything but follow you.

## Game Film: Zuora Ignites a Movement— Transforming a Market

I've long been an admirer of Zuora, the self-proclaimed leader of the "Subscription Economy," a term they have actually claimed as a trademark. I admire their foresight in identifying a *big* trend, and their courage to stake their success around it. In 2008, when Zuora first emerged, they had a vision and they executed on it; results were encouraging early on, which was noted in their blog (with emphasis by me) on December 29, 2008: "By the end of the year, *our vision of the subscription economy* and the power of on-demand billing and payments had resonated with more than 60 customers. 2008 was good to us."

Fast-forward a mere seven years later (as Jason Lemkin of SaaStr recently pointed out, B2B SaaS is a 7–10 year journey to $100M), and they have parlayed this early success into a *huge* business that promises to have spectacular returns to investors. In short, Zuora has started a movement!

Within market movements, we see the constant bubbling up of new flashmobs, parades, and the spawning of new movements. Leaders find ways to create flashmobs, get in front of parades, and parlay their successes to build movements.

Many name Salesforce.com as the pinnacle of market leadership—the leader of a movement. Bubbling out of the Salesforce SaaS/CRM movement, Zuora established itself as the add-on subscription billing solution. From there, Zuora focused nearly 100% of its marketing on becoming *the* thought leader on the Subscription Economy. If you cared about subscription businesses, you cared about what they said. This is the quintessential strategy of parade leadership.

Now, the Subscription Economy is everywhere, and Zuora's product line and ambitions have grown with it. It no longer markets subscription billing, and it has even moved past subscription accounting and management to what it calls "Relationship Business Management," which is described as "commerce, billing, finance for any company and every industry."

I expect to see from Zuora—as an aspiring leader of a new movement—some of the following as it continues its march toward what is certain to be a very profitable IPO:

1. An increased focus and visibility for its partner program and partner success, which while robust, is a small link in the footer of its website today
2. An opening up of its platform via an API, a developer program and a third-party marketplace
3. Several senior executive hires and additions
4. An increasingly contentious relationship with co-travelers like Netsuite and Salesforce.com

I have no doubt that Zuora is on a path to success. They understand the dynamics of today's market and how content, thought leadership and execution foster leadership.

● ● ● ● ● ● ● ● ●

We can now use the Market Leadership Lifecycle to accelerate our Breakthrough Marketing journey. We do this by clearly identifying our market leadership objectives based on where we are in that lifecycle, and then use that to define our objectives and fine-tune our messages and our messaging mix. Let's take a look at each of these steps.

## Identifying Your Market Leadership Objectives

Are you catalyzing a Flashmob, running to the front of a parade or starting a movement? How will you measure success for each of these goals? Here are some ideas depending on your market phase.

### Flashmob: Market Creation

At this point in our market-leadership journey, we are building our initial Flashmob of customers. These customers care first and foremost about solving an immediate problem, and while they do live in a context, they are primarily solution seekers. We win the communication battle by articulating the value of our Better Mousetrap.

- Communication Objective: Deliver unique insight
- Business Objective: Customer acquisition and referenceability
- Key Metrics: New logos, referrals, references, customer-value delivery
- Key Audience: Problem owner/solution implementer
- Messaging Mix: 70% Value (feature/benefit); 30% Viewpoint (business context)

## Parade: Market Leadership

In this phase our goal is to emerge as the leader of the new market segment. There are many new "mouse traps" for buyers to choose from. We must elevate our message to be almost 50% related to Viewpoint and Purpose, from pure value to the problem solver, to helping the P&L owner in their journey to success. This is perhaps the hardest transition to make, as many companies cling to hard to value. But the rewards are great, as those who succeed rise above the crowd and win more, grow faster and increase customer and shareholder value.

- Communication Objective: Alignment of Viewpoint with customer's strategy
- Business Objectives: Customer acquisition and customer success; establish thought leadership
- Key Metric: New logos, renewal and repeat purchase; visibility PR metrics on thought leadership platform
- Key Audience: Functional or key P&L owner
- Messaging Mix: 40% Value (feature/benefit); 50% Viewpoint (business context); 10% Purpose (destination)

## Movement: Market Transformation

Companies that create a Flashmob and then transform themselves into a market-parade leader have the rare opportunity to define a movement. Movement-definers go beyond Value and current context to changing and transforming the market, not just for their solution, but also for other complementary and related ones. They create business platforms for partnership and communications. Their messaging is not only about Value and context, but also about shared purpose with their customers.

- Communication Objective: Inspiration
- Business Objectives: Ecosystem building, product-line expansion, market expansion
- Key Metrics: Revenue growth, valuation, market-share expansion
- Key Audience: Executive
- Messaging Mix: 20% Value (feature/benefit); 40% Viewpoint (business context); 20% Purpose (destination)

## Market Leadership Phase and Messaging

We often talk about the "wisdom of the crowd," which is a concept to be understood and reckoned with, especially in investment and other information based products. But here I want to talk about "wisdom *for* the crowd" in B2B markets. After all, building a crowd of customers is what B2B sales and marketing teams must do. And knowing what kind of crowd you are going after—flashmob, parade or movement—is critical to getting your messaging mix right between Value, Viewpoint and Purpose.

As you move from market creation to market leadership to market transformation, your message mix shifts from Value to Viewpoint to Purpose and your audience grows from Problem Owner to P&L Owner, to C-level. But what are Value, Viewpoint and Purpose messages? Let's take a quick look at these definitions.

**Value Messages**: Messages that connect directly to the business value of your product and are typically one of five types:

1. Cost Savings
2. Increased Revenues
3. Risk Reduction (including compliance)
4. Business Agility
5. Innovation Improvement.

You can solve a lot of technical, tactical and other problems for clients, but if you can't connect these problems to quantified business values, the size of your crowd will be very small indeed. Not only that but we should strive for *Unique* Value, one that is not obtainable elsewhere, and then you are on your way. This of course requires an intimate knowledge of not only customers and their problems and opportunities, but a clear understanding of available substitutes and alternatives to your solution.

**Viewpoint Messages**: Also referred to as "story types," these are messages that have strategic impact on your customer's bigger issues beyond the scope of your solution. As there are five types of Value messages, the four types of Viewpoint messages are:

1. **Trendspotting**: This messaging names and frames an environmental shift that is either keeping the customer up at night or creating great opportunities for them. *Example: Zuora and the Subscription Economy*

2. **All Pain, No Gain**: This messaging focuses on the pain of trying to solve today's big, known problems with yesterday's solutions. This works great when the pain is large enough to induce action and is well recognized and acknowledged yet unaddressed. *Example: FireEye and Advanced Threat Protection*

3. **Better Mousetrap**: This messaging takes advantage of situations when a customer is spending money to fix a problem, but has either not eliminated the problem, or the cost of doing so is too high; this leads with, "Hey, what you have stinks and I've got a better solution here." This Viewpoint works great in replacement markets. *Example: Palo Alto Networks and "It's Time to Fix the Firewall"*

4. **Brave New World**: This type of Viewpoint describes the promised new state if the customer implements your solution.

It's powerful because it talks about the intersection of the customer's world and your unique solution. *Example: Skyhigh Networks and "Rethink Cloud"*

**Purpose Messaging**: These messages reach high above transforming the P&L of your business to transforming the industry or even the world. Used with appropriate care and at the right time, purpose messaging can accelerate your business and leadership and help you transform the market you are in. There are three types of purpose-based messaging:

1. **Business Transformation**: We will change the way the business world runs. *Example: Salesforce.com and the "End of Software"*
2. **Business Inspiration**: We will change the way you think about things. *Example: Zappos and "Delivering Happiness"*
3. **Societal Transformation**: We will change the way the world works. *Example: Google and "Accessing the World's Information"*

### Market Influence and Messaging Mix Across the Market Lifecycle

Your messaging mix and delivery has a dramatic impact on your potential to influence the market. This is shown here in Figure 26, which illustrates the potential of market influence corresponding to your messaging implementation.

Typically, organizations start with product messages to establish presence in the marketplace. This is the natural starting point, especially in situations with technical founders solving well-defined problems from their experience.

Quickly, these product founders realize that their product is not meaningful in the broader market. They then realize that they must add value messages in order to move from mere market presence to having meaning to customers in their target market. Hopefully, they have read

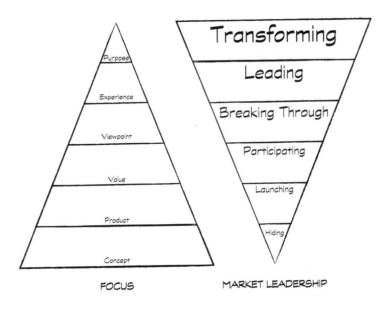

Figure 26: Messaging and Leadership Potential

Chapter 7 so that their Value messages are unique and rise above the many problems with Value outlined.

Unfortunately, even if they get Unique Value right, most organizations stop there. They may be valuable and have meaning to a small group of customers, but they fail to truly impact the broader market segment they operate in. As we have seen, if we add an aligned Viewpoint to our messaging, we can then achieve actual impact on the market by beginning to tilt the playing field to our advantage and actually influencing the Value perception of customers. Hopefully by now you have a firm understanding of how to build your Viewpoint Story and impact your market.

As we saw in Chapter 9, if we then deliver these messages with experience and engagement, we increase the velocity of our programs and are able to Breakthrough and begin to truly lead the market. And finally, once we add purpose to our mix, our leadership and influence increases so much that we begin to form an ecosystem and movement around our solutions, and in the process transform the market and potentially even the world. In fact, we can now layer our Flashmob, Parade and Movement phases on this messaging-leadership diagram, shown in Figure 27.

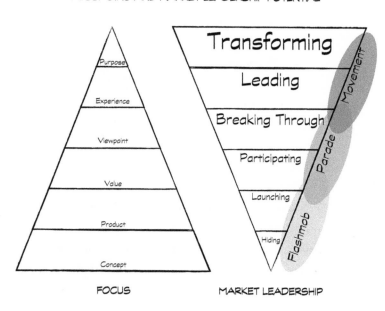

Figure 27: Messaging, Leadership and Market Phases

As we see, our messaging type does not correspond 1:1 to our market phase; rather, it's a messaging mix, or weighting, that changes over time. Let's take a look at each phase and the reason for the mix of messaging, the benefits of this messaging mix and the risk of getting the mix wrong.

When we are in the early market creation, or Flashmob stage, we are very focused on the problem owner. Our messaging is primarily value-based, focused on the problem we solve and the value of doing so. However, we must still spend some of our energy on context or Viewpoint. As we have seen, without Viewpoint, it is harder to get noticed and be in the game. If we allow established vendors to own the context with buyers, there is simply no room in the market for innovative solutions. During this phase, start with the challenge and quickly transition to your Value. Spend 70% of time on Value and 30% on Viewpoint.

When we transition to the market leadership or Parade phase, we must spend more time challenging buyers with our unique Viewpoint. Because we have likely exhausted the "easy buyers" who are directly attracted to our Value message, we must spend more time and energy getting the attention of the next tier of buyers. Often, we must appeal strategically to the problem owner's boss, the P&L-level executive. Our Viewpoint content goes to about 40% before we drop into Value. We must get alignment in our messaging to the strategic objectives of the P&L owner. In this phase, if we have it articulated, we can also start talking about our transformational purpose messaging, but do so lightly and only in executive-targeted channels and programs.

If we are lucky enough to reach the transformation, or Movement phase of market ownership, our value messaging takes a back seat to our Purpose and Viewpoint. Our purpose becomes the meta-context of our shared Viewpoint with the executive and P&L owners, and we only drop into value discussions in active selling or in marketing targeted at problem owners. However, as we begin to reach higher we must remain grounded and become adept at smoothly transitioning between these three tiers of messaging.

One size does *not* fit all; some markets are ripe for creation and transformation while others are more stubborn and may require movement forming earlier than usual. Fortunes can be made by doing a great job of market creation with a heavy emphasis on Value and just a bit of Viewpoint. However, recognizing where you are or aspire to be in this lifecycle is critical to getting your Purpose/Viewpoint/Value messaging mix correct.

## CHAPTER 15

# MARKET LEADERSHIP UNCORKED—
# A FIVE-STEP PLAN

**S**ome B2B markets take off slowly while others seem to come out of nowhere to disrupt and change their market. Many are 10-year "overnight" successes. And while many of the same trends we've been discussing in this book are tending to collapse market creation time, there is still a natural cadence and rhythm to market disruption and leadership.

Regardless of whether we are innovating in an existing category, creating a new complementary solution, or consolidating the spend from multiple categories, we are still faced with the need to create and lead our segment and eventually—if we are both skilled and a little lucky—to transform our market. However, the challenge, as we have seen, has never been greater. Competition is everywhere; buyers are fiercely independent and inundated with information, so vying for their attention—let alone successfully marketing and selling to them—is increasingly difficult.

By adopting the Viewpoint, Value and Experience approach outlined here, we can Breakthrough and win. To succeed in this journey we advise a simple, five-step plan.

1. Shift Your Mindset
2. Identify Your Market Leadership Objectives
3. Create Your Viewpoint
4. Articulate Your Value
5. Double Your Experience

Let's take a look at each of these.

## Step 1: Shift Your Mindset

Technology products are amazing things that change our world; however, many great technologies never reach their potential because when brought to market by technologists, they get mired in the "wow, that's cool technology" mindset. The engineer proudly shows and describes every feature, algorithm, bit and byte in painstaking detail while he thinks: "Isn't my baby beautiful?" And while this may be interesting to a small number of highly technical users, it fails when the buyer steps in and asks the simplest of questions: "Why should I care?" We must shift our mindset from "Isn't my baby beautiful?" to "Isn't your (the customer's) world amazing?" Former Netscape CEO Jim Barksdale said (loosely paraphrased), "We don't live for profit, we live to *thrill* customers." Thrilling customers by changing their world for the better is at the core of the Velocity Marketing Mindset. When you live to thrill customers, your entire world lens is theirs. In other words, Viewpoint starts from the eyes of the customer. Value is described in their terms and delivered in the context of their experience. So the first step is to decide to thrill and serve customers, not to do cool features.

## Step 2: Identify Your Market Leadership Objectives

Are you catalyzing a Flashmob, running to the front of a Parade or starting a Movement? How will you measure success for each of these goals? As we've discussed, we then use this decision to define our communication and business objectives, our audiences and key metrics, and then build our messaging mix accordingly. Table 2, on the next page, recaps this discussion.

## Step 3: Create Your Viewpoint

Regardless of where you land in the market-leadership lifecycle above, you need a well-articulated and powerful Viewpoint. Get the team together and use the AIM STEEP framework to build your Viewpoint Story. Do it today!

## Step 4: Articulate Your Unique Value

Articulate and document your Unique Value. Share it widely within the organization and test it with customers to refine it. Drive both your communications and product roadmap around these key, Unique Values.

## Step 5: Double, no... 10X Your Experience

Run an audit of your marketing communications against the two dimensions of engagement and experience discussed in Chapter 11. Are you heavy on low-engagement, low-experience web pages, whitepapers and data sheets? Probably. You must *demonstrate* your Unique Value early and often in the buying process. Figure this out and you can unlock velocity you never imagined was possible. Leverage your product, expertise and data to do this—but get it done!

| | Communication Objective | Business Objective | Key Metrics | Key Audience | Messaging Mix |
|---|---|---|---|---|---|
| Flashmob | Unique Insight | Customer Acquisition, References | New logos, referral leads, endorsements | Problem owners and solution implementers | Value: 70% Viewpoint: 30% |
| Parade | Strategic importance | Accelerated customer acquisition and success | New logos, Renewal and repeat purchase PR metrics on thought leadership | Functional and key P&L owners, C-level sponsors | Value: 40% Viewpoint: 50% Purpose: 10% |
| Movement | Inspiration | Ecosystem, product line and market expansion | Revenue growth, valuation and market share growth | Executive | Value: 20% Viewpoint: 40% Purpose: 20% |

Table 2: Market Leadership Objectives By Phase

Once we have completed these five steps it is critical to execute them with consistency, veracity and ferocity. What does this mean?

**Consistency** -*Reliability or uniformity of successive results or events.*

Telling a story once isn't enough; telling it over and over again is what creates Breakthrough and notice. Over how many years and how many times did Marc Benioff of Salesforce.com show up with the "No More Software" logo? The first time it was eye catching; the second time it became interesting; and the hundredth time it was compelling because everything he said was a riff on this theme. You were a believer and you came along for the ride.

**Veracity**-*Correctness or accuracy.*

Every time they tell the story they back it up with supporting and compelling facts, data and figures! FireEye cranks out a ton of research to support their "Next Generation Threat Protection" story. They are the experts and they back it up by sharing that expertise—all the time!

**Ferocity**-*The state or quality of being ferocious, marked by unrelenting intensity.*

To be believed you yourself must be a true believer. You can't fake ferocity, and if you don't have it, then your story will never have the impact of those who do.

Organizations that are stuck in the Launch and Participation stages of market leadership can expect to convert, at the most, one lead per hundred to revenue, and more typically half of that. However, by following my Breakthrough Marketing approach, you will move from Launching to Leading at a minimum of 6x improvement in marketing ROI in as little as six months. So be ferocious and consistent and back it up with real facts, and you too can deliver impactful, Breakthrough Viewpoint- and Value-based stories and messages. You will Breakthrough, Lead and Transform your market, thrilling customers and building a valuable and lasting company. I wish you a successful and fulfilling journey from Launching to Leading and beyond.

# APPENDIX

# BREAKTHROUGH MARKETING MODELS AND FRAMEWORKS

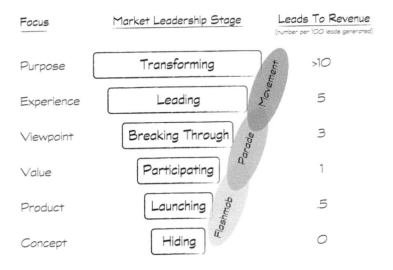

MARKET LEADERSHIP ACHIEVEMENT LADDER
BEYOND MARKET LEADERSHIP

| Focus | Market Leadership Stage | Leads To Revenue (number per 100 leads generated) |
|---|---|---|
| Purpose | Transforming | >10 |
| Experience | Leading | 5 |
| Viewpoint | Breaking Through | 3 |
| Value | Participating | 1 |
| Product | Launching | .5 |
| Concept | Hiding | 0 |

The Extended Market Leadership Journey;
See Chapters 1, 3 and 13 for Discussion

## THE MODERN MARKETING RACECAR

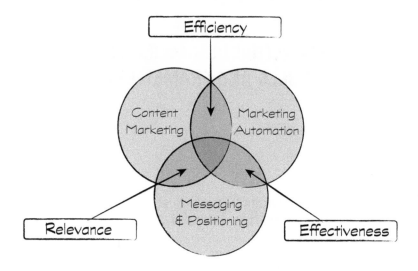

The Modern Marketing Racecar; See Chapter 1 for Discussion

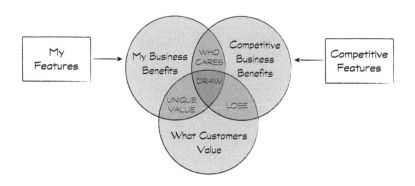

Unique Value; See Chapter 4 for Discussion

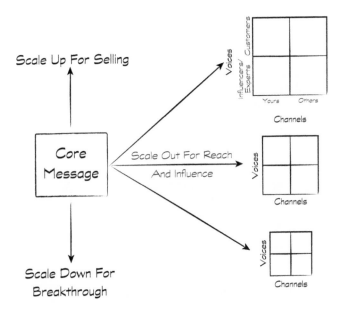

Scale Up For Selling

Core Message

Scale Out For Reach And Influence

Scale Down For Breakthrough

Message Scaling Roadmap; See Chapter 5 for Discussion

THE VIEWPOINT STORY WHEEL

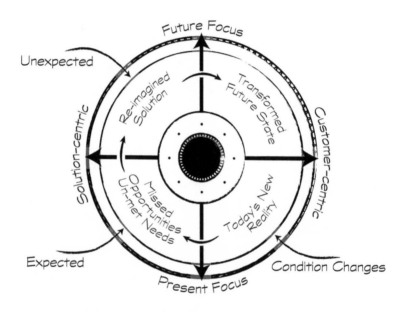

The Viewpoint Story Wheel; See Chapters 6, 7 and 8 for Discussion

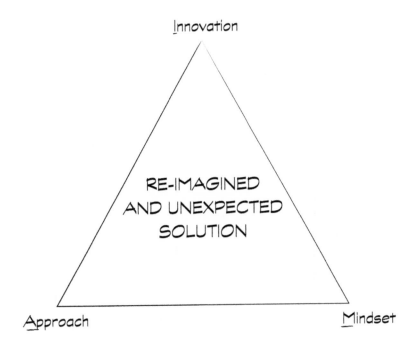

Figure 15: The AIM Solution Framework; See Chapter 7 for Discussion

THE VIEWPOINT STORY MATRIX

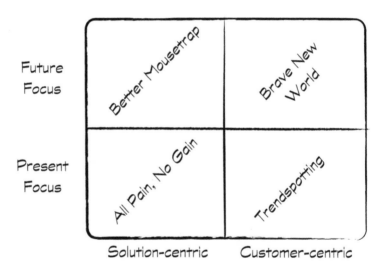

The Viewpoint Story Matrix; See Chapter 8 for Discussion

## THE VIEWPOINT STORY CHOOSER

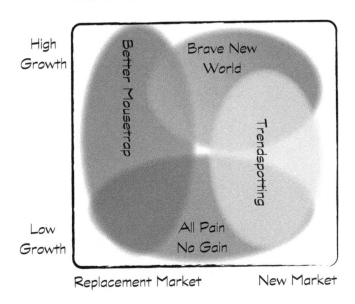

The Viewpoint Story Chooser; See Chapter 9 for Discussion

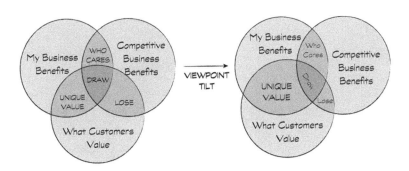

Viewpoint Tilts the Playing Field; See Chapter 10 for Discussion

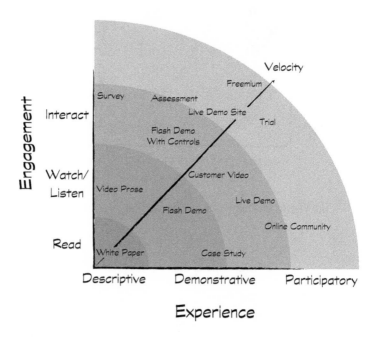

EXECUTING WITH VELOCITY

Engagement and Experience Create Velocity; See Chapter 11 for Discussion

MESSAGING AND MARKET LEADERSHIP POTENTIAL

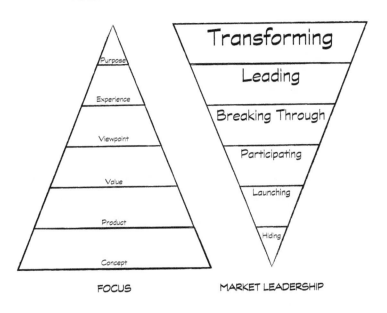

FOCUS         MARKET LEADERSHIP

Messaging and Leadership Potential; See Chapter 14 for Discussion

# ACKNOWLEDGEMENTS

First and foremost, I want to thank all of my clients, past, present and future; without you there is no business, no ideas and no book. Thank you for letting me be of service to you, I truly cherish the opportunity to help; it is a great honor and privilege.

Writing a book is no small undertaking. I've been writing this book in fits and spurts since 2010. But in September of 2015 it was starting to feel like my version of "Mr Holland's Opus" with no real commitment or end in sight. That's when Peter Cook said to me "just finish the book and bring it to Sydney in February, no excuses." Pete, thanks for kicking me in the backside and getting me moving, teaching me about motivating myself, and for believing in my journey and me.

Thanks to Matt Church for teaching me how to express my ideas in powerful and meaningful ways. Without Matt's teaching, this book would not exist. Matt's influence is sprinkled throughout, including my focus on context. Matt introduced me to the power of models and metaphors, and much much more. And thank you to all of the fellow travelers I have met through Matt and Pete's Thought Leaders Global community. The Thought Leaders tribe is amazing in its support, openness and innovation, and I am humbled to call them my friends and colleagues. And of course a special shout out to Donna McGeorge who introduced me to this amazing group of thinkers, doers and leaders.

In creating this book, four people made huge and lastly contributions to the quality of the words and images. First, my editors Michelle Phillips and Jessica Ehlert. Michelle was instrumental in helping to shape the lump of clay into a well structured story. Not only that, she pushed consistently to make the book better, going beyond the call of editor. Without Michelle, there would be no Viewpoint Story Wheel, which is the creation in the book I am the most proud of. Thanks Mish! Jessica Ehlert was meticulous and relentless in her edits to make the book readable and understandable. Thanks Jessica. If Mish inspired the Story Wheel, Lizziee Jerez made it come to life. All of the myriad of drawings and models look great because of Lizziee's work. The three of you took the fat caterpillar of a book and transformed it to a beautiful butterfly, thank you so much for the help. Also to Vince Vasquez, who was generous and invaluable to me, introducing me to his Cloudbook team of Jessica and Lizziee and providing sage advice on the whole process of "finishing" the book.

Besides writing the book, there is the publishing of it. Learning the "book business" can be intimidating for a first time author like myself. Thanks to John Willig, Mel Abraham, Becky Robinson and Dan Markovitz who all provided advise, introductions, resources and counsel to me that made the journey a success, leading me to my eventual publisher, Morgan James. Thank you to Terry Whalin, David Hancock, Margo Toulouse, Nickole Watkins, Jim Howard and the rest of the Morgan James team for a great partnership.

With a career of three decades behind me, I've learned from and been supported by so many great colleagues, clients and advisors that I am sure I will leave someone off of this list, so to you I am sorry, if you feel left off, let me know and I will buy you a beer! Thank you to the following: From Northwestern; Scott Halstead, John Nealon, Scott Singer, Steve Johnson, Mike Johnson, Jim Degan, Mike Mehlmann, John Huber and the late Jeff Helfer, who have been lifelong friends and supporters. From IBM; Scott Frandsen, Terry Rombalski, and Fred Schmitz. From Intel; Karen Alter, Dennis Carter, Ellen Konar, Deb Conrad, Lakshmi Pratury, Sally Fundakowski, Joanne Chan and of course the late Andy Grove. From Netscape; Jen Bailey, Jane Smith, Jerrell Jimerson, Julie Herendeen, Lynn Carpenter, Greg Sands, David Pann, Atri Chatterjee, Susie Wyshak, Kurt Wedel, Judy Logan, Jim Barksdale, Barbara Werner, Lori Rose Yurtin, Kristina Homer Armstrong, Jody Kramer, and many more, not the least of which is the late Mike Homer. Others friends, colleagues and fellow travelers who must be mentioned include in no particular order; Richard Prest, Aron Chazon, John Mahlmeister, Sandra Mahlmeister, Matt Fairbanks, Marty Ward, Chip Krauskopf, Glenn Helton, Paige Alloo, David Macey, Robin Pederson, Peter Chung, Peter George, Kurt Bertone, Sara Papas Hillman, Rishabh Mehrotra, Brian de Haaff, Andrew Gray, Jim Greene, Bob Roblin, Mitch Tuchman, Colin Savage, Dave Mohr, Brian Spector, Pat Moran, Tom Grubb, Jeb Miller, Asheem Chandna, Phil Kazuba, Roman Stanek, Blaine Mathieu, David Gee, Gary Read, Phil Lin, Scott Brinker, Varun Kholi, Elaine Cummings, Burt Cummings, Karen Halstead, Susan Thomas, Jamie Lerner, Ross Fuji, Tom Caldwell, Veenu Prashar, Sam Muaddi, and Kate Healy. Whether you know it or not, you have all played a part in making this book a reality, so thank you.

And lastly to my wife Joel' and my four amazing kids. There are not enough love, kisses and hugs I can give to thank you for everything.

# SOURCES AND NOTES

All trademarks, logos and brands mentioned in this book belong to their respective owners; no rights are claimed or implied in their fair usage.

## Pre-game

Introduction: In 2012, Gartner first predicted that CMO spending would exceed CIO spending by 2017. With 2017 fast approaching it's hard to prove or disprove this prediction. But the point is really moot. There is no doubt that marketing organizations are voracious adopters of technology, and this is changing the way marketers deliver programs and measure results.

Game Film FireEye: FireEye is a great company that executed just about as well as one can. The work we did together was exciting and innovative and the FireEye story is one I am grateful to have played a small part in.

## Game Plan

<u>Game Film Bear and the Alligator</u>: The Microsoft Windows 95 launch event may have marked the zenith of Microsoft's influence over and dominance of the computing industry. Being in Redmond for the event is a vivid memory for me. We were fighting a valiant fight, and it surely stoked my competitive fires. The subsequent history of Netscape and Microsoft are well documented, but I hope this adds one small story to that history.

<u>Chapter 1</u>: The term Content Marketing is used in its broadest sense, the processes, people and programs that bring messages into the market. While the term is new, in many ways marketers have been doing this since the first advertisements centuries ago. Technology has increased the channels of communication and lowered the cost of both content creation and distribution, but has not yet replaced the art of what and how to say things.

<u>Chapter 2</u>: Fig 3, 4 and 5. Source A16z.com/portfolio and subsequent Google searches

<u>Chapter 2</u>: CEB quotes 57% statistic often on their website, www.cebglobal.com

<u>Chapter 2</u>: Scott Brinker's website is a great resource, Fig 6 is from here: www.chiefmartec.com/post_images/marketing_technology_landscape.jpg

<u>Chapter 3</u>: For more on lead to revenue and other metrics see blog.marketo.com/2012/10/the-roi-of-marketing-automation.html and other entries at the Marketo blog

<u>Game Film: Velocity Football</u>: Sports Illustrated; September 17 2009, Jon Wertheim, and Scorecasting September 2011. For more on Kelley see the HBO Real Sports story of January 2012.

## The Opening Drive

<u>Chapter 4</u>: I have a love hate relationship with Value. This is probably pretty obvious from the titles of the chapter and the subsequent Coach's Corner. Value is critical to get right, and I love that. But if we overvalue value, we get lost in a world lacking context and meaning. I hope this book strikes the right balance between valuing and overvaluing Value.

<u>Chapter 5</u>: I love the Marvel superheroes, and make no claim to them at all, but it's great to pretend to have their superpowers every once in a while, and I thank them for the help in this chapter!

## The First Half Playbook

<u>Coach's Corner, Chasm What Chasm?</u>: As I say in the Coach's Corner, Moore's book is amazing and incredible. I can only hope that this book has 10% of the impact that his did. However, I do think it has gotten a bit dated. In fairness, Mr. Moore has written other books and has incredible insight into technology markets. I hope my critique has hit the right chord of respect and criticism.

<u>Game Film: Cirque Du Soleil</u>: What can I say, Cirque is amazing. Business wise, creative wise, and joy wise. I chose to include this story because it is such a strong example of the power of context and creativity.

<u>Chapter 8</u>: FireEye, Palo Alto Networks, Zuora and Virgin America are four great companies who are leading their market parades, all in different ways. It is a privilege to profile them in this chapter.

<u>Coach's Corner: The Hero's Journey</u>: Joseph Campbell was an amazing thinker and a prolific writer. His influence is so widespread that quoting him can risk being a cliché. However, the analogy was so powerful for me that it rose above cliché to meaning. If you put one non-business book on your reading list, make it The Hero With A Thousand Faces.

<u>Chapter 10</u>: Covey's work like Campbell's is amazing. If there is one concept from this chapter that is underplayed and underdeveloped,

it is Abundance. If you do a great job, competition takes care of itself. There is an ABUNDANCE of business out there. Focus on your Value, Viewpoint, and execution, and competition will take care of itself.

## The Second Half Playbook

Game Film: Nimsoft on Demand: CEO Gary Read and Nimsoft were my first consulting client, and I owe much of my success to them. Nimsoft was a fabulous client and we did great things together. The Unified Monitoring strategy was one of the best. Gary pushed and pushed to make this a reality, and in turn pushed my thinking on what can get done and how quickly you can do things. Thanks Gary.

Game Film: Something Quirky: Granata Pet Food Video www. youtube.com/watch?v=t8dmjoqOOQo

Game Film: Something Quirky: Sun Valley Skippy Video vimeo. com/62259357

Chapter 13: Tom Grubb and Scott Brinker are two leaders in the marketing automation world. I highly recommend both of them to help you navigate technology and automation challenges.

## The Final Drive

Chapter 14: You probably never heard of DMTI Spatial before you read this book. Phil Kazuba and his team did a great job at changing the market context and igniting a new Flashmob that created customer and shareholder value. Phil was invaluable in helping me to document that success.

Chapter 14: I've never done work for GoodData or Zuora, but they are both great role models of the Viewpoint in this book. A special thanks to both organizations for being supportive of this book in small but meaningful ways.

# ABOUT THE AUTHOR

Ken Rutsky is a B2B marketing consultant focused on helping his clients breakthrough and become market leaders. Ken has spent nearly 25 years in B2B marketing roles, launching the Intel Inside broadcast co-op program in 1994 and then the Internet's first affiliate marketing program, Netscape Now, while at Netscape from 1995–99. Since then, Ken has been the CMO at several start-ups and ran network-security marketing at McAfee, where he developed and executed a marketing strategy that grew its web security business from $60M to nearly $200M.

Today, as KJR Associates, Inc. Founder and President, Ken leverages his knowledge from his extensive Silicon Valley career to help his clients lead their markets. Ken has honed his Breakthrough Marketing framework with successful implementation at dozens of client companies including FireEye, Nimsoft, Sophos and more. In the seven years in his practice, Ken's clients have generated more than $6B in shareholder value through IPOs and acquisitions. In addition, several others have reached private equity valuations of more than $1B. A past contributor to CloudExpo Journal and Cloudbook, Ken is a well-regarded speaker and blogger, having presented at conferences including SaaS University, CloudExpo, the RSA Conference, and many other user groups, meetups and events.

Ken has an engineering degree in Material Sciences from Northwestern and an MBA from Stanford. Ken is married and has three beautiful daughters and one awesome son. When he isn't working, you can find Ken driving his kids to practices, rehearsals, games, plays and other school functions, or running around in his yellow, soccer-referee shirt. When he has time, Ken loves to take his road bike for a long, hilly ride.